THE YOUNG MAN'S
GUIDE FOR
PERSONAL SUCCESS

Edited by Linda Ellis Eastman

Professional Woman Publishing
Prospect, Kentucky

THE YOUNG MAN'S GUIDE TO PERSONAL SUCCESS
Copyright © 2008 by Linda Ellis Eastman
All rights reserved.

Published by:
Professional Woman Publishing
Post Office Box 333
Prospect, KY 40059
(502) 228-0906
http://www.prowoman.net

Please contact the publisher for quantity discounts.

ISBN 13: 978-0-9799711-2-9
ISBN 10: 09799711-2-8

Library of Congress Cataloging-In-Publication Data

Cover Design and Typography by:
Sential Design, LLC — www.sentialdesign.com

Printed in the United States of America

Dedicated to Albert Henry Eastman
for his lasting impact on all who have met him

TABLE OF CONTENTS

TABLE OF CONTENTS
-CONTINUED-

TABLE OF CONTENTS
-CONTINUED-

ABOUT THE AUTHOR

LINDA EASTMAN

Linda Ellis Eastman is President and CEO of The Professional Woman Network (PWN), an International Training and Consulting Organization on Women's Issues. She has designed seminars which have been presented in China, the former Soviet Union, South Africa, the Phillipines, and attended by individuals in the United States from such firms as McDonalds, USA Today, Siemens-Westinghouse, the Pentagon, the Department of Defense, and the United States Department of Education.

An expert on women's issues, Ms. Eastman has certified and trained over one thousand women to start consulting/seminar businesses originating from such countries as Pakistan, the Ukraine, Antigua, Canada, Mexico, Zimbabwe, Nigeria, Bermuda, Jamaica, Costa Rica, England, South Africa, Malaysia, and Kenya. Founded in 1982 by Linda Ellis Eastman, The Professional Woman Network is committed to educating women on a global basis regarding, self-esteem, confidence building, stress management, and emotional, mental, spiritual and physical wellness.

Ms. Eastman has been featured in USA Today and listed in Who's Who of American Women, as well as Who's Who of International Leaders. In addition to women's issues, Ms. Eastman speaks internationally regarding the importance of human respect as it relates to race, color, culture, age, and gender. She will be facilitating an international conference where speakers and participants from many nations will be able to discuss issues that are unique to women on a global basis.

Linda Ellis Eastman is also founder of The Professional Woman Speakers Bureau and The Professional Woman Coaching Institute. Ms. Eastman has dedicated her businesses to increasing the self-esteem and personal dignity of women and youth around the world.

Contact
The Professional Woman Network
P.O. Box 333
Prospect, KY 40059
(502) 566-9900
lindaeastman@prodigy.net
www.prowoman.net
www.protrain.net

INTRODUCTION

Linda Ellis Eastman

Young men are facing stressful situations on a daily basis involving relationships, school, dating, job searches, and self-identity. There is increasing pressure from today's society to "be a man" and oftentimes confusion about what it really means to be a man.

This book is written as support and guidance for young men and their families. It is authored by consultants, coaches, and professionals who have shared such tips and strategies as increasing self-esteem, setting personal goals, handling anger and frustration, learning to forgive and money management.

Young men today are filled with hope and determination. This book is designed to help overcome the roadblocks and hurdles which are presented on a daily basis.

THE YOUNG MAN'S
MAN'S

GUIDE FOR
PERSONAL SUCCESS

ABOUT THE AUTHOR

KIMBERLY M. DAYE, M.ED.

Kimberly M. Daye is both driven and passionate about her calling to serve youth, women, and families. With over 11 years experience, her pursuits have been primarily in the field of education where she has focused on youth empowerment and leadership as well as public health with emphasis on health and wellness. Ms. Daye has served as an educator and leader in the non-profit sector managing several programs as project coordinator, curriculum developer, and grant writer to senior operations director. Most recently, Ms. Daye is building a training division for her current employer while leveraging her skill set as a consultant, insightful public speaker, dynamic workshop/ conference facilitator, and trainer for a host of organizations, churches, and businesses.

Ms. Daye is a graduate of the University of Pittsburgh with a Bachelors degree in Behavioral Science & Africana Studies and Regent University where she received a Masters of Education in Educational Leadership. Her educational achievements are balanced with numerous certifications and training merits ranging from Strategic Planning to Abstinence Education. Ms. Daye is a member of the Greater Philadelphia Chapter of the American Society of Training and Development (ASTD), the Professional Woman Network (PWN), the Urban League of Philadelphia, and the Joseph Alliance, Inc., where she has served on the mission field in ministry in Ghana, West Africa.

As a woman of God, mentor, visionary, and entrepreneur, Ms. Daye is determined to impact the nations for the Kingdom of God. Her fervor in serving the Lord has led to ministry appointments in arts/ dance ministry, community outreach, service to ministry leaders, and missions work where she served with a team to set up a village based wellness clinic, women's conference, and outreach to youth orphanages. She is currently establishing the launch of an international consulting firm in near future. The *Young Man's Guide for Personal Success (For Teenage Boys & the People Who Love Them)* is her first publication and is soon to be followed with her second co-authored release, *Emotional Wellness for Women, Vol. 1* by Professional Woman Publishing.

Contact:
Kimberly M. Daye
Philadelphia, PA 19122
Email: walkinginpurpose@yahoo.com

ONE

EMPOWERMENT & PURPOSE: YOUR MISSION IS POSSIBLE

By Kimberly Daye, M.Ed.

"Those who say it can't be done are usually interrupted by others doing it."

The Spirit of Empowerment: "What Are You Gonna Do?"

Several years ago I was given an assignment to work at a youth program that changed the very course of my life and my way of thinking. I had worked with youth all my life and was hired to work as program director. Like any other assignment, I was excited to organize, inspire, and make an impact and difference in the lives of youth as I always had. It was the first day. I walked into the site, looked to the left, and saw a group of youth sitting on gym bleachers; young men sitting, talking – some laughing – some shoving each other. I thought to myself, this must be a mistake. How could I possibly be in the right place with so many boys? While it was true that I had worked with male students in the past, I had never exclusively worked with males, particularly teen males. My first thoughts were to walk away, thank the director for giving me the opportunity, and let her know that indeed she had made a mistake. So I proceeded to turn around, and as I was leaving, a young man said, "Hi... you must be new. Are you staff?" I hesitantly replied "yes." He introduced himself and said, **"We've been waiting for you. Now what are you gonna do?"** I said, "I will do what I came to do." What that young man didn't know is that he had empowered me. He caused me to make a decision. He asked me a question that I had to answer, and challenged me in the area that I thought was out of my league. You see, all my prior experiences led me to that point. The choice was mine; to either take the easy route and leave, or stay and learn. That night I brainstormed the plan and proceeded. As I reflect back on that assignment, it inspired me to seek purpose for my life. I felt empowered to make a difference in the lives of others.

The spirit of empowerment meets you where you are. (At its root, it comes from the word empower, which is to give power, or authority, to promote the influence of….. www.merriamwebster.com). That which is put in front of you will either empower you to take action or no action at all. It will give you release or authority to move. It asks you, "What are you going to do?"

So, how do you respond? What action do you take? How do you know what to do? How do you know it aligns with your purpose? And what is "purpose", anyway? So glad you asked! Stay with me for a moment and let's examine the tools we've been given. Yes, given. You see my friend, we all have purpose and a true mission to fulfill. No matter how big or small, it exists.

In the popular *Mission Impossible* series, Ethan Hunt receives instructions for an assignment that is virtually impossible for the average man to complete. You see, Ethan has been trained, equipped with the latest in technological devices to complete the mission, and is skilled to navigate through the most difficult obstacles with success. Upon hearing the assignment, he is told that the assigned instructions for this mission will self-destruct in seconds, and he therefore must listen carefully and closely. As he listens, he is rarely reminded that he has the tools to complete this mission, but is expected to complete the assignment without failure. After several challenges, near-death feats, and overcoming the most unusual mishaps, he completes the mission and is soon gearing up for his next assignment, which is likely to be more difficult than before. Like Ethan, our journey through life will be filled with ups and downs, twists and turns, and insurmountable obstacles, but we can overcome them all. You may ask how, but I assure you that you've been given the tools to write your own story. In the meantime, I'd like to share seven mission principles to guide your steps.

Mission Principle #1: Listen Closely...There Is a Divine Plan For Your Life.

"True empowerment is knowing that you are living your divine purpose: that which is designed only for you."—Kimberly Daye

You may have heard some of the key empowerment phases such as: "Be all that you can be, son. You are the author of your own destiny." Or even the ever-popular "A mind is a terrible thing to waste." Perhaps your parents, relatives, teacher, coach or pastor have drilled these things into your head. Maybe you've even said these phrases to others or yourself. These are words of power and encouragement spoken to give inspiration and guide you. But is there a roadmap to steer you! Where do you start? You start with YOU!

Take a moment and think about what actually inspires you. What gives you that spark, that real motivation, and drive? What do you really enjoy? Think about it… Now, write it down. Keep it at the forefront of your mind and determine to do it. Not there yet? Let's go a step further.

Before you were born, God decided that you would be a part of this world. He formed and crafted everything about you. He intricately designed you and all your experiences (wins, losses, ups, downs, ins and outs) and decided that you would leave a mark on this world at this specific time. When He created you, He created you with significance to play a role in this life and to impact time. The details and everything concerning your life, whatever your package (small, large, Black, White, Latino, Asian), whatever your make up, you are here for a specific purpose. With the package, He has already equipped you with the tools needed for success. You are empowered and given the license to live out the very purpose that He has created for you. Whatever the size, from the greatest athletes and public figures, to the janitor who cleans your school, it is significant, and it is only for you.

Got you thinking a bit? Good! Take a moment and list some things that interest you.

Interests:

_____

_____

_____

Keep this list close. You may feel inspired to make changes. Review your list; you may be that much closer to uncovering your purpose. My friend, it's a journey. As you learn more about yourself and your interests, you will need time to learn, practice, and grow in the very thing that interests you.

Mission Principle # 2: Your Talent Is Genius; Study and Learn It Well.

"To do easily what others find difficult is talent; to do what is impossible for talent is genius." —Henri Amiel, www.giga-usa.com/quotes/authors

So, you've at least indentified your interests. What are you good at? Look at your list and write the first thing that comes to mind when thinking about what you are really good at:

_____

_____

_____

Okay. So let's also list a few things that you may want to *become* good at:

_____

_____

_____

You're getting there. It is important that you take the time to develop your talent. You must practice, practice, and practice some more. The greatest athletes take the most time disciplining themselves to eat right, exercise, and even study... yes, study! They study videos of others who are excelling in their field. There are times when they even study themselves to understand their strengths and weaknesses and how to improve upon them. The key is to be a student of what you are passionate about so that you can be the best at it.

I met a young man years back that truly inspired me. He was about fifteen and wanted to become a better writer. Oddly enough, his writing skills at first were not so good. However, with much practice, he got better. He went a step further and not only did he grow to become a wonderful writer, he also became an awesome public speaker. He is now a college student attending school on full scholarship! Whatever you aspire to do, be good at it and do it well. Decide to map out a course of action for yourself and follow that plan. This leads us to the next principle to help you plan.

Mission Principle #3: Create and Fine Tune Your Blueprint.

> *The best way to predict the future is to invent it.*
> —Alan Kay, www.smalltalk.org

You may be thinking, "Okay, plan what?... and with what $$$?" That, my friend, is why you must draft your goal plan or blueprint. Having a print of your plan will help guide you in your process of becoming a man of action.

What if your teacher came to school unprepared and confused about what you were going to be taught that day? Or perhaps your favorite sports team had no strategy or plan to win a game. It would become very difficult to know which direction to move in or what to do next. This is why drafting a plan of your ideas is important. As things happen, you are able to go back to your plan and adjust where needed. With each adjustment, be careful to stay focused on your goal, and be sure that every adjustment aligns with your goal. Consider the sample plan below:

A Plan for Success *Inventing Your Future*		
Short-Term Goals	**Goal #1**	**Blueprint:** How will you get there? What steps should you take? **Help:** Who can help chart your plan?
	Goal #2	**Blueprint:** How will you get there? What steps should you take? **Help:** Who can help chart your plan?
	Goal #3	**Blueprint:** How will you get there? What steps should you take? **Help:** Who can help chart your plan?
Long-Term Goals	**Goal #1**	**Blueprint:** How will you get there? What steps should you take? Where will you start? **Help:** Who can you turn to for advice?
	Goal #2	**Blueprint:** How will you get there? What steps should you take? Where will you start? **Help:** Who can you turn to for advice?
	Goal #3	**Blueprint:** How will you get there? What steps should you take? Where will you start? **Help:** Who can you turn to for advice?

Mission Principle #4: When Trouble Comes, Do Not Fear, Stay The Course.

Don't let negativity given to you by the world dis-empower you.
Instead, give to yourself that which empowers you."
—Les Brown, www.wow4u.com/lbrown/index.html

Far too often we have great ideas, get a plan of action in place, set the course to achieve our goal, and the minute trouble (adversity) enters, we run. It is this very thing that so easily throws us off course and keeps us from achieving our best. Can I tell you that many times I've started things and have been completely discouraged at the very thought of opposition? Can I further be honest and say that I did not even bother to write anything on paper because of this very fear. Sure it would be nice for everything to be smooth sailing with no problems, but the reality is that part of the equipping process that I mentioned earlier means that you have been equipped for the challenges, too. You must not allow negativity or any trouble to discourage you from completing what you have been created to do. Truly, it's much easier said than done, but the point is that it can be done. Allow yourself to focus on what is motivating you or empowering you for the mission. How do you do this? For every negative statement or reason you can think of for not achieving something, replace it with a positive! You must choose to actively cancel out negativity. Consider every negative thought that could come your way and create an attack plan to capture the negative thought. Here's one way:

Reasons I CAN'T...	Reasons I CAN...
I'm too young.	Who says?
I'm too small.	Everyone starts somewhere.
What do I possibly know about_____?	I have been preparing myself.
Too difficult; it can't be done.	It can be done.
What a dumb idea. Besides, someone else has already done____.	I've been purposed to this.

Now write a few of your own:

Reasons I CAN'T...	Reasons I CAN...

The truth is that you must learn to encourage yourself. The people who don't believe in you are doing their jobs: *acting in the seat of opposition so that you can't grow stronger and more determined.* You must exercise staying connected and focused on your mission. It helps to build the experience required for you to learn how to overcome obstacles, failures, and defeats. Growing in this way helps you learn how to put "haters" in their place, and appreciate them for helping you get that much closer to your goals. Positive application of this concept helps to develop character. This is also excellent practice for progress toward your next mission principle, humility.

Mission Principle # 5: You Must Be Humble; Your Mission Is Much Bigger Than You.

"It is not what he has or even what he does which expresses the worth of a man, but what he is." —Author Unknown.

Your success in achieving your mission is based upon more than just reaching your goal. You must consider how you got there, what you used, and how you actually achieved it. Sure, Michael Jordan is one of the greatest basketball players of all time, but one day someone may not remember that. What they might remember is his technique and how he grew to become one of the greatest. They may be interested in the skills he used and how they can take those skills and use them to improve themselves. Everything you do is more about the process and how you can help others. This is what makes your mission bigger than you. You must humble yourself and be respectful. This is the path towards gaining respect. Everyone is concerned about being disrespected; but the truth is that respect is earned. You don't have to worry about making someone do this… they will because of your character. If you humble yourself and give respect, people who may not even like you will respect you. So, because your mission is bigger than you are, there is no way you can give up.

Mission Principle #6: Whatever You Do, Do Not Give Up!

"It is not because things are difficult that we do not dare;
it is because we do not dare that things are difficult."
—Seneca, www.followyourdreams.com/courage.html

There was a group of young men determined to win a contest. The prize was regional recognition for the most original youth leadership project. For two years straight they competed, but did not win. In year three, they tried a different strategy. This time they involved their friends (those that were truly like-minded), assigning each of them specific tasks. They met each week to discuss their progress and continued to pull together as many resources as possible. In the end, the project was more successful than it had ever been! And, at the regional convention, what happened? They did not win. Why? How did they miss it this time? The answer is that they didn't miss it at all. They surpassed it! The regional convention was great, but it was at the *national convention that they received recognition for one of the "most original" campaigns.* Their determination caused them to surpass what they thought was as high as they could go and catapulted them to a national level. My friend, it's as simple as this: if at first, second, or even third you don't succeed; try again. If it's purposed for you to do it, then it will happen. Maybe not exactly the way you pictured it, but it will happen. Sometimes your rewards are packaged much differently than how you imagine! To that degree, you must never give up. You must allow yourself to dream big.

Mission Principle # 7: Dream Big!

"Some men see things as they are and say, 'Why?' Dream of things that never were and say, 'Why not?'"—George Bernard Shaw

One day, I decided to make a list of things I wanted to accomplish during my lifetime. I came up with about eight on my personal list. Several years later (which was actually about five months ago) I had to make another list. One of them from my list is happening this very moment... to share my experiences with you. I am a dreamer, and I have a book by my bed where I record my dreams when I wake up each morning. Today, I encourage you not to be afraid to dream BIG!!!!

Final Thoughts

"If you think you are too small to be effective, you have never been in bed with a mosquito." —Reese

"The person who removes a mountain begins by carrying away small stones." —Anonymous

My dad said to me, "You have big dreams to build, sure. But did you ever stop to think that before you can build, you must first learn how to mix the cement (the foundation)? That is one of the most important things you can do. So as you build, you are building on a foundation that will stand." My friend, I want to tell you that I am building. I've had to overcome frustration, fear, impatience, and my own self-defeating ideas and ways of thinking. While overcoming these obstacles, I realized this had been part of strengthening my foundation; that which actually existed before I was even born. Whenever your moment comes, you must remember that you have been purposed for something great! As you read these lines, wherever you are, YOU are attached to destiny and you have been empowered for your purpose. So I say to you, as a very influential young man once said to me… **"I've been waiting for you. Now what are you gonna do?"**

Love You and God Bless!

Recommended Reading:
The Holy Bible:

- *Boys Bible (NIV)* by Rick Osborne, Author

- *NIV Revolution: The Bible for Teen Guys.* Livingstone Corporation

Holla Back...But Listen First: A Life Guide for Young Black Men by Mister Mann Frisby. (Skye Larieux Publishing, 2006)

Letters to a Young Brother: MANifest Your Destiny by Hill Harper. (Gotham Books, 2006)

The Pact by Sampson Davis, George Jenkins, Rameck Hunt & Lisa Frazier Page. (The Berkley Publishing Group, 2003).

The 21 Irrefutable Laws Of Leadership: Follow Them and People Will Follow You by John C. Maxwell. (Thomas Nelson Publishing, 1999)

ABOUT THE AUTHOR

JOHN LOBLACK

John Loblack is originally from the tiny Caribbean Island of Dominica. Prior to migrating to the US, John worked as a government information officer. In that position, he was fortunate to have traveled throughout the Eastern Caribbean, and Taiwan.

Since moving to the U.S.A. in 1993, he has earned a bachelor's degree in sociology and a master's degree in human resource development. In June 2008, John will graduate with a doctoral degree in organizational leadership. In the US John has worked in all aspects of food service, and has taught in elementary, middle, high school, and at a private for-profit institution. Currently, John runs Goalmind Coaching & Consulting, LLC, a learning and performance company he started in 2006. John is a professional speaker and an author of one book, *Mental Entree.*

Non-professionally, he is an avid sports fan, poet, soccer player, father, son, brother, and civic minded citizen. John is a passionate reader of professional development, and has been a member of the Central Florida Chapter of the American Society of Training and Development, Central Florida Chapter of the Society of Human Resource Management, Central Florida Chapter of the African American Chamber of Commerce. John Lives in Wesley Chapel, Florida with his wife Marilyn.

Contact:
Goalmind Coaching & Consulting, LLC
(813) 532-4375
goalmind@johnloblack.com
www.johnloblack.com

TWO

GOAL SETTING: GETTING FROM A TO Z

By Dr. John Loblack

Can you remember your days as a child? Do you remember all the fantastic things that you said you would do, be, and have? Have you accomplished any of those fantastic things? Congratulations to you if you have reached at least one of the many things you promised yourself as a child! If, however, if you have not yet fulfilled any one of these dreams, why not? Can you identify the reasons why you failed to fulfill those dreams? Could your failure be attributed to the fact that you paid too much attention to the outside voices; the voices that kept telling you that you never would do this or that you and would never amount to anything in life. My guess is that you allowed the **dream killers to steal your dream**. It is, however, not too late to turn that around. This time, you must promise yourself to work to fulfill that which you set on your mind and heart. In fact, the purpose of this chapter is to teach you how to set and accomplish your goals.

Goal Setting

Goal setting is simply a way to get over all your limitations successfully. But how do you set and accomplish goals? Zig Ziglar says that a goal is like a target. Consequently, to hit a target one must first have a target at which to aim. If one looks at a target in the same light as a destination, one might conclude that there might be more than one way to reach that target. For example, if one's destination is New Mexico, one might decide one might decide to use plane, train, or automobile to get there. No doubt, the amount of time one has would determine the mode of transportation that one uses to get there. The same is true for goals. Time by way of a deadline is a critical component of goal setting. There is, however, more to goal setting than identifying a target and setting a deadline. Let's begin.

Take a sheet of paper and write the word "GOALS" at the top of the paper. Number the paper 1 through 30. Then, write without stopping the things that you would like to do, be, and have over the next ten years. Fill the entire page, and then put the paper aside. We'll come back to it later. Congratulations! You have completed your first goal setting task by writing the thirty things that you would like to focus on the next ten years of your life on. You might be saying to yourself, wait a minute. It can't be that easy. Yes! It is that easy. All that's needed is to apply a tried and proven formula to help you along the way. That formula spells **SMART** formula. It stands for Specific, Measurable, Action-Oriented, Realistic, and Time Centered. A new formula, **RARE**, will also be introduced to you. That formula will help you solidify your SMART efforts to set and accomplish your goals.

Be Specific

Circle the answer that you think most accurately answers the following question.

What is the first question you would ask your best friend who asked you to join him on a long road trip?

    a.   When are we going?

    b.   How much will it cost?

    c.   Where are we going?

    d.   None of the above.

If you are like most people, you probably chose "C". It is the best choice because it influences everything else. In other words, it is easier to reach a goal when it is clearly identified, **specific.** The more specific the goal, the easier it is to identify the resources that you would need to fulfill it. For example, which is easier to save: a lot of money or $10,000? Saving $10,000 is easier because it is countable; it means the same thing to everyone. A lot of money, on the other hand, means different things to different people.

So, looking back at the thirty goals that you set at the beginning of the chapter, choose your ten most important goals and ask yourself these questions, "Are these ten goals specific, and would they mean the same thing to anyone who looked at them?" If your answer is no, you should rewrite them and make them as specific as possible. For example, if one of your goals was a Caribbean vacation, rewrite that goal by identifying the Caribbean island(s) that you would like to visit on your vacation. If another of your goals was to be a professional athlete, rewrite that goal by stating whether it is football, basketball, baseball, and so on.

Measurable

To describe a goal as a well-written goal, one must be able to measure ones progress toward its attainment. Against that background, it would be easy to understand the need for that goal to also be specific. One cannot measure vague goals, but specific goals can be. It is easy to evaluate your progress toward accomplishing a goal to save $1,000, but not quite that easy to evaluate your progress toward saving "a lot" of money. The same is true if one's goal is to lose 100 pounds, to run a marathon, to earn a bachelor's degree in sociology, or to become a professional football player. With this in mind, I would like you to revisit your top ten goals and evaluate them on the grounds of their measurability. How are you going to determine your progress? What are you going to use to determine how close you are to reaching your goal?

Using your top ten goals, write one sentence explaining how you will evaluate your progress. For example, "I'll know that I am getting close to reaching my goals by counting the amount of money that I have saved"; or "By evaluating the amount of miles that I run on a weekly basis." Whatever it is, write it down so that you'll know what you are working with. You could answer that question by writing a series of questions like this one:

I will know that I am reaching my goal (when) _____ .

Action Oriented

To fulfill the SMART formula, all goals must include the taking of some kind of action. For example, if your goal is to have in your possession $1,000 by December 25, 2008, you must do one or more things to secure that money. These action steps could include working for that money and saving a specific amount each month or each week. If your goal is to participate in a marathon, the action steps would include running a set amount of miles each week in preparation for the marathon. Choose three of your top ten goals that you have identified and complete the following sentences:

1. The action steps that I need to take to reach my goal is

   _____

2. The action steps that I need to take to reach my goal is

   _____

3. The action that I need to take to reach my goal is

   _____

Realistic

In addition to being Specific, Measurable, and Action oriented, all goals must be realistic. They, however, must be realistic to the individual goal setter. It would be very difficult for anyone to be motivated to fulfill someone else's goal. It is normal for one to find inspiration in someone else's story, but the goals that one sets should be a reflection of how that individual feels about what he/she wants. No one knows you better than you do! Therefore, **you** are the only one to determine the kinds of goals that you would like to pursue. If you set them, your own goals would drive you to do what it takes to fulfill your goals.

Complete this exercise before moving forward. Review the goals that you wrote at the beginning of the chapter and choose your top five goals. After doing so, complete the following statement:

1. *The action that I must take in order to reach my goal is:*

_____

2. *The action that I must take to reach my goal is:*

_____

3. *The action that I must take in order to reach my goal is:*

_____

4. *The action that I must take in order to reach my goal is:*

_____

5. *The action that I must take in order to reach my goal is:*

_____

Time Frame

Goals without a deadline are merely dreams; therefore, you must attach a deadline to your goals. The time frame that you set is entirely up to you, but it would be helpful to set short-term, medium-term, and long-term goals. Short-term could be goals that you would like to achieve within the next three to six months. Medium-term goals could be the kind of goals that you would like to reach within the next year to three years, and long-term goals are the type of goals that you would like to attain within the next five to ten years. So, is there a mix of short-term, medium-term, and long-term goals in your top 10 goals? Study them now and make that determination. You don't want to set yourself up for failure; therefore, you should ensure that you attach *realistic* time frames for the attainment of your goals.

For example, if you are a junior in high school and you want to become a medical doctor; that would be a long-term goal. If, on the other hand, you are a junior in high school and your goal is to graduate high school with a 3.5 GPA in June 2008; that would be a short-term goal. An example of a short-term goal for you (as high school junior) would be acceptance at the college of your choice upon graduation from high school.

Now that you understand the value of deadlines, use the ten goals that you have identified and rewrite them with the appropriate time frames. It would be to your advantage to write those goals in the present tense. Write them like you are achieving them today. Here are a few examples:

1. *Today is December 31st, 2008, and I am earning $100,000 a year.*

2. *Today is June 30th, 2008, and I am weighing 225lbs.*

3. *Today is May 9th, 2008 and I am completing the last chapter of my second book.*

4. *Today is December 31st, 2017, and I am making my last mortgage payment.*

Now, it's your turn. Use the format below or develop the kind of format that best fits your personality.

Today is_____ and I am doing _____ .

Today is_____ and I am earning _____ .

Fantastic, you are now well on your way to reaching your goals. You have done what 97% of the adult population fails to do. The rest is up to you. **Remember, the dictionary is the only place where success comes before work.** Keep planting in your mind the kinds of seeds that will lead you to the fulfillment of your goals. You, however, must guard against the goal killers who will appear from all corners to dissuade you from working towards your goals. Always believe in yourself, and always surround yourself with people who might be going in the same direction as you. Make use of time instead of allowing time to make use of you and the results will take care of themselves. That leads me to the RARE formula. That formula forces you to stay on course when the detractors try to steer you away from your goals. Like the SMART formula, each letter in the word RARE represent a pillar in the goal-setting process.

Review

From time to time it might be necessary to review your goals. For some reason, the results that you anticipated keep eluding you. Revisit your goals; they might have been unrealistic from the start. If you conclude that they were unrealistic, then it's time to rewrite them so that they would now be more realistic. Sometimes, too, life happens and you were unable to invest the time, effort, and money that you originally wanted to invest. When you find yourself in that predicament, rewrite your goals.

Adjustments

Things seldom work in ways that we anticipate; consequently, we must make the adjustments when life throws us a curve ball. Goal setting and achievement is no exception. Making adjustments, therefore, can make the difference between success and failure. Don't be stubborn; change directions if the road that you are traveling is not taking you in the direction that you want to go. Adjustments could be in changing the goal from short-term to medium-term, or from medium-term to long-term. It could also mean the giving up of a goal entirely. So, after reviewing your goals make the adjustments, if adjustments would make the difference.

Responsibility

You have invested the time to set your goals; now, you must take responsibility for your success or failure. No one owes you anything; therefore, you owe it to yourself to do the work to reach the goals that you have set. Taking responsibility means that you will not make excuses if and when things don't turn out the way you initially planned. Taking responsibility means doing the research to arm yourself with the information that you need to hit the target that you have set. Taking responsibility means investing the time, effort and money to reach your goals. Failing to take responsibility for the attainment of your goals warrants the time invested in setting the goals a waste of time.

Enjoy The Process

If you were not enjoying the process, it would feel like torture; therefore, you need to do all that you can to enjoy the process. People achieve more when they are having fun, when they are enjoying what they are doing. The reverse is also true. People's production diminishes when they are not enjoying what they are doing. If you don't believe me, ask anyone who wakes up every morning to go to a job that they do not like. It is much easier for you to achieve your goals if you enjoy the process; therefore, let your hair down and go have some fun in achieving your goals. As Zig Ziglar says, "I'll see you at the top."

Notes:

_____

_____

_____

_____

_____

_____

_____

_____

_____

_____

_____

_____

_____

_____

_____

_____

_____

_____

_____

_____

_____

ABOUT THE AUTHOR

TONYA MOORE

As a successful empowerment speaker, writer, and Training Consultant, Tonya has been commended for playing a major part in changing the lives of both young men and women locally and nationally.

She has been given the name "Encourager", for inspiring individuals to soar above obstacles and think outside the box. As a motivational speaker Tonya has had the opportunity to share spiritual and professional guidance through her seminars and workshops. She is a Certified Youth Trainer, Certified Professional Speaker, and Certified Training Consultant in Diversity and Women's Issues.

Tonya is the President and CEO of The Eagle's Nest Development Network, an International Consulting Organization which is geared towards the Professional and Spiritual Development for Youth and Women. She is also a member of the Professional Woman Network (PWN) and the National Association of Female Executives (NAFE). She is a contributing author for the book, *The Young Man's Guide to Personal Success*. Tonya has over 15 years of experience working in Corporate America, where she currently serves as an Associate Fixed Income Portfolio Trade Assistant at Harris Investment Management, Inc. She is a licensed and ordained minister as well as a former youth director with over 10 years of experience in Christian Education Facilitation. She received her degree in Business Administration from Indiana Institute of Technology and continues theological biblical studies at Trinity International University.

Contact:
Eagle's Nest Development Network
230 S. Clark Street # 170
Chicago, IL 60604
773-260-0247
info@endn.org
www.endn.org

THREE

OVERCOMING PERSONAL OBSTACLES

By Tonya Moore

Andy was very excited about the thought of entering high school. As a gifted mathematician, he dreamed of becoming an entrepreneur building luxury homes. His mother, one of his greatest fans, supported him 100%. She decided to submit an application for him to attend the Robert Jones Magnet School. On the day of Andy's eighth grade graduation ceremony, the Dean made a special announcement before his family and peers that Andy had been accepted into Robert Jones Magnet School. His family was overjoyed, but his classmates were shocked and angry. They began teasing him and flipping spitballs on the back of his head. As Andy proceeded to the stage to accept his award, he held his head down, dragged his feet, and remained silent. After leaving the graduation, he was saddened and surprised by the actions of his "so called" friends.

While on summer break, Andy was harassed. He began receiving prank calls, eggs were thrown at his mother's car, and empty beer bottles were tossed into his yard. He couldn't walk down his own street without being picked on and sometimes kicked or pushed down by his classmates. Andy was mistreated because he was a gifted student and accepted into a great school. After a while, Andy had had enough and decided he just wouldn't go to Robert Jones. Afraid to tell his mother, he began school anyway. At Robert Jones, Andy made every effort to fail. Eventually, he was kicked out of school for not maintaining the required GPA. Andy ended up right where his so called friends wanted him, at the school with them. Did this make any sense at all on Andy's part? What could he have possibly gained by making a decision like this? Could Andy have handled this differently?

Obstacles

An obstacle is defined as anything that seriously hampers action or progress. When something is *allowed* to slow us down, or stop us from reaching our goals, dreams, desires or overall potential in life, it's an obstacle. We end up losing while that obstacle wins. We've given that "something" too much POWER! Andy allowed himself to be controlled by his peers, causing him to lose focus of his God-given purpose in life.

Emotions

How did Andy lose focus? He lost focus by giving into a fear. Everything starts with a thought, and then there's an action taken based upon that thought. Our overall destination is determined by how we deal with our thoughts and emotions. I like to think of an emotion as an underlying catalyst of how we react to certain issues such as with anxiety or nervousness, just to name a few. Our emotions, if not dealt with, can become personal obstacles. In order to overcome our obstacles, we must first have a desire to discover our **personal emotional barriers.**

Emotional Barriers

As humans, we all face personal obstacles that can stand in the way of our success. Those personal obstacles are considered emotional barriers. There are five areas of emotion that we will cover briefly. Fear, failure, negative attitude, insecurity, and un-forgiveness all play a major role in how we deal with our obstacles. The following is an exercise that may familiarize you with emotional response.

Exercise:

Beside each one of these emotional barriers, choose the response that best describes the reaction to the specific feeling:

FEELING	RESPONSE
1. Fear_____	A. Resentful
2. Failure_____	B. Complain
3. Negative Attitude_____	C. Worry
4. Insecurity_____	D. Non-Achiever
5. Un-forgiveness_____	E. Unconfident

If you noticed, some of these emotions are interchangeable with the descriptive feeling.

Fear

Fear can keep us from enjoying everyday life and fulfilling our purpose. Dr. Paul A. Hauck, PhD, author of *Overcoming Worry and*

Fears says, *"When you are afraid of something and you consciously know what it is that you are afraid of, that is fear."* For an example, if you were told that you failed your final exam and the semester was ending, your natural reaction might be to worry and be fearful as to whether you would pass the class. You were aware of what made you afraid.

Two of the most common fears are rejection and fear of failure. These two fears are considered more powerful than any of the others, because we tend to go through great measures to avoid challenges and opportunities. We fear that we may fail, and people will reject us if we do. It's like a roadblock that stands in the middle of the road stopping us from getting to the other side. By identifying your fear, you can begin the overcoming process. Once identified, you can create a plan that will gradually get you motivated and courageous enough to take a risk, reveal yourself, and chance what you fear most.

The following is an exercise that may help you delve into your fears.
I fear_____

Write down five ways you think may be helpful with overcoming your fear.
1. _____
2. _____
3. _____
4. _____
5. _____

Failure

Everyone fails. We all have to deal with it at some point in our life, but we can overcome it. When we don't achieve the desired end result, we fail. Here are a few reasons we fail.

1. Holding on to childhood pain

2. Lack of focus

3. Resistance to change

4. Impatience

5. Poor planning

6. Fear of the unknown.

If I were to rank these reasons from one to ten, fear of the unknown would be number one. When fear is allowed to control our destiny, it most often leads to failure. You overcome when you plan to succeed, and learn from your mistake(s) without allowing failure to infiltrate. If you allow failure to live inside of you, it will hibernate and eventually take root.

Write down any failures that you've faced in your life.
I failed at_____

Write down five ways you think may help you overcome failure.

1. _____
2. _____
3. _____
4. _____
5. _____

Negative Attitude

There are many reasons negative attitudes overshadow our personality. A negative attitude causes one to be mentally subservient to thinking and walking in defeat. We are not confident in our own powers or abilities. Complaining becomes normal conversation when communicating. If a negative attitude is not dealt with, it can lead to depression, stress, and poor health. It's our attitude that determines our success or failure in life. To overcome is to think and speak positively. It's important to learn how to focus on the good things in life. Communicating with positive people, building self-esteem, and believing in yourself will help create a positive attitude.

Write down things that cause you to have a negative attitude.

I have a negative attitude because _____

Write down five ways you believe are ways to overcome your negative attitude.

1. _____
2. _____
3. _____
4. _____
5. _____

Insecurity

According to Joseph Nowinski, PhD, author of *The Tender Heart-Conquering Your Insecurity*, insecurity is *"a profound sense of self-doubt, a deep feeling of uncertainty about your basic worth, and your place in the world."* When in self-doubt, we tend to be more aware of what people are thinking, making it difficult for us to socialize and get involved in conversations with peers without thinking that someone is talking about us. Insecurity depicts a negative judgment of self and a deep concern of how others perceive us. We lack confidence and sound decision-making, our feelings are easily hurt, and we tend to withdraw ourselves from others. We are more vulnerable to being controlled and taken advantage of. Identifying that these problems exist is the beginning of overcoming insecurities. Do a self-test by writing down different things that describe your insecurities and, one day at a time, work through the list becoming more conscious of those areas, and slowly make changes to improve.

Write down what makes you insecure.
My insecurity is _____

Write down five ways you believe would be a good way to overcome your insecurity.
1. _____
2. _____
3. _____
4. _____
5. _____

Un-Forgiveness

Un-forgiveness is when we choose not to extend forgiveness. This is a bitter, unfruitful, and unhappy way to live. We hold on to hurts and grudges. It's important to forgive and renounce any desire to get even, in order to begin healing. We must release past hurts from our mind, meditate often, and pray for the offender. Holding on to un-forgiveness doesn't allow for progressive movement in life. Peace will be difficult because that situation will torment you the rest of your life, leaving no room to rest or be free in your mind. You are bound to it unless you let it go.

Write down any un-forgiveness.

I have un-forgiveness toward _____

Write down five ways that may be a good way to overcome un-forgiveness.

1. _____

2. _____

3. _____

4. _____

5. _____

Overcoming

Overcoming is allowing healing to come to fruition. There must be a desire to change and release each barrier; this is vital to your success in life. Being able to recognize and identify what it is and understand how it took root can bring about change and deliverance to your mind, soul, and spirit. Be honest with yourself by asking the "do I" questions: "Do I become offended easily?" "Do I have a negative attitude?" Taking time to be real with yourself will help defeat any obstacle. You're admitting the obstacle might be present, by choosing to take a risk and to conquer it.

Success

Making reasonable and realistic goals is crucial to being an achiever. Begin by establishing an action plan and sticking to it. Don't let anyone define who you are and what you will become. Never be passive with your hearts desires, but take an aggressive approach and go after them. One of my favorite quotes is, *"Wanting something is not enough. You must hunger for it. Your motivation must be absolutely compelling*

in order to overcome the obstacles that will invariably come your way."
—Les Brown.

Personal Statement

Allow this to be your personal statement for the rest of your life.

Personal Statement
I _____ have overcome _____ and I will no longer take my eyes off my goals. but will look for windows of opportunity to succeed. I am victorious. I can be whatever I want to be, have whatever I say I can, and go wherever my eyes take me. I will stand against opposition, face my fears, and persevere through difficult times. I will embrace my achievements and learn from my mistakes. I_____am an overcomer of personal obstacles. Signature_____ Date_____

Frame this declaration and hang it in your room, your locker, or wherever you feel is a good place to remind you that you will never be bound or held back from anything as long as you live. If you live for today and plan for tomorrow, you will receive a bright and peaceful future.

ABOUT THE AUTHOR

Micki K. Jordan, MLDR

Micki Kremenak Jordan is a mentor, trainer and coach. She has held a variety of corporate management positions over the past 25 years. She has participated on Visioning and Strategic Planning Teams, Leadership Teams and in Training and Development of staff.

Micki has a Bachelor of Science Degree in Sociology from the University of Iowa. After several years in the corporate world she obtained her Masters of Arts in Leadership from Bellevue University, Bellevue, NE. Micki is certified in Diversity Training, Public Speaking and Professional Coaching and holds the Certified Insurance Councilor Designation. She is a member of the Professional Woman Network (PWN) serving on their International Advisory Board and the National Association of Female Executives (NAFE).

Her passion is assisting others to recognize their true potential. She has written chapters entitled "Living Your Values" and "Mirror Image", that may be found in the PWN publications *"Women's Survival Guide for Overcoming Obstacles, Transition and Change"* and *"Women's Journey to Wellness: Mind, Body & Spirit."* She also has chapters entitled "Super Vision" in the book *"Overcoming the Superwoman Syndrome"* and ÁRE YOU a Shadow or a Light" in *"Women as Leaders: Strategies for Empowerment & Communication".* All books are part of the PWN library.

This chapter is dedicated to her son, Chad, a young man well on his way to success. She is very proud of his accomplishments, his work ethic and above all his character. While having a distinct personality of his own, he sets an example for others in his ability to make solid decisions in a position of leadership. He demonstrates that *"people grow through experience if they meet life honestly and courageously. This is how character is built"* – Eleanor Roosevelt

Contact:
Micki K. Jordan
863 Gleamstar Ave.
Las Vegas, NV 89123
(702)463-5786
www.protrain.net
mk.jordan@yahoo.com

FOUR

MACHO MAN: THE IMPORTANCE OF CHARACTER

By Micki K. Jordan

It's All About Character
Watch your thoughts, they become words.
Watch your words, they become actions.
Watch your actions, they become habits.
Watch your habits, they become character.
Watch your character, it becomes your destiny.
— Frank Outlaw

What is Character?

Everyone comes into this world with the same opportunity to develop a commendable character. You are not born with character; it is not hereditary. It is something that you and only you have total control over its development. You are born with the potential for building any type of character you choose, good or bad. *"Parents can only give good advice or put them on the right paths, but the final forming of a person's character lies in their own hands."* – Anne Frank

Your character is not your reputation. Abraham Lincoln said, *"Character is like a tree and reputation like its shadow. The shadow is what we think of it; the tree is the real thing."* Your reputation might be the "Macho Man" with an exaggerated sense of strength, it may be that you are a "Geek" or a "Nerd" or a "Loner" or whatever label that has been placed upon you. Your reputation is what others think about you. Your reputation may or may not accurately reflect your actual character. William Hershey Davis says, *"Reputation is what you are suppose to be; character is what you are…. Reputation comes over one from without; character grows from within."*

Character is described in several ways. H. Jackson Brown, Jr. said, *"Our character is what we do when no one is looking."* It may be said that it is living from the inside out. It has no race, no religion, no education, no gender, and no specific personality. As Rev. Dwight Moody said, *"Character is what you are in the dark."* Character is:

Courage. This is the desire and ability to do the right thing and not the popular one. It is following your conscience and not the crowd. It does not mean the absence of fear, but the ability to face it.

Humility. The ability to know you are not the most important person in a group. You need to have confidence in your abilities, while knowing there is more to learn and more you can improve.

Attitude. Your words and actions show how you feel about certain events. It is how you express yourself about tasks you must do; how you face challenges and obstacles you may encounter. It directly effects whether or not you will be successful. It may be positive or negative.

Responsibility. It is being accountable for your actions and your thoughts. You are considered reliable, dependable, and committed to completing an obligation or a task. You do not blame others for things that may happen, nor do you take credit for work that is done by someone else.

Accepting. You are able to look at individual differences in appearance or beliefs without prejudice. You have the ability to recognize the uniqueness and value of each individual you meet. You judge others based only upon their abilities, their actions, and their words.

Caring. You are concerned about others. You are kind, helpful, compassionate, and forgiving. You are able to show your feelings to others and help people in need.

Trustworthy. Honesty is always the best policy. Others believe in you and trust you because of who you are, someone worthy of this trust. If you make a promise, you will keep it. You follow through on your obligations.

Enthusiasm. You are excited about the things you are involved with, and it shows. This indicates you are interested and care about people and issues. It contributes to a positive attitude and can be contagious among others.

Respect. This is important in how you relate to others, how you regard their feelings, and is the attitude you reflect. It is treating others in the same manner you want to be treated. This is a very big part of your character.

Key Elements of Good Character

Character is something we develop, it is learned. It is the pattern of our behavior or our habits. We are often unaware of why we do or say things in a particular manner. Building one's character is the process of acquiring ethical and moral standards. The American Dictionary of the English language defines it as *"the stable and distinctive qualities built into an individual's life which determine his response regardless of circumstances."* It needs to be understood that everyone <u>has **a** character</u> of some sort or another. It also needs to be understood that not everyone <u>has character</u>. Every choice that is made is a step towards developing the kind of person you choose to be.

The following are several more key words that may be used to describe your character. Think about the words on the list and how they would apply to your character.

- Awareness – knowing what is going on around you.

- Attentiveness – showing interest in others and in activities.

- Commitment – having the follow-through to do what you say you will.

- Communication – the ability to properly exchange information, both giving and receiving.

- Compassion – aware of other's issues, an understanding and a desire to help.

- Confidence – being confident of abilities and beliefs; self-esteem.

- Consideration – thoughtfulness of other's feelings and beliefs.

- Cooperation – a willingness and ability to work with others.

- Courage – the ability to face fear and to accept the unknown.

- Creativity – looking for new ways to accomplish or improve things.

- Decisive – able to make a decision and to stick with what you think is right.

- Dependability – others can count on you to follow through on your commitments.

- Determination – the ability to stick with a task no matter how hard or impossible it may seem.

- Discipline – in control of your thoughts and actions; self-control.

- Effort – the willingness to try, even if it is something you are not very good at doing.

- Fairness – looking at all sides and making the right decision for everyone involved. It is following a balanced standard without regard to one's own feelings.

- Faith – having belief without proof in a positive outcome, believing in your abilities, and a belief in God or other higher being.

- Focus – able to concentrate and avoid distractions.

- Forgiveness – willingness to accept others (and your own) mistakes and move on past the issue.

- Generosity – the act of giving of yourself in some way to the benefit of others.

- Honesty – you do not lie, cheat or steal from others. Always being truthful, even when it is difficult to do.

- Initiative – the ability to get started without having others telling you what needs to be done.

- Integrity – your code of honor, your values and beliefs.

- Kindness – being nice to others.

- Loyalty – faithfulness to others and to issues, even when it is difficult and not a popular view.

- Motivation – what causes you to take action.

- Optimism – having a positive outlook.

- Patience – the ability to wait for things to happen, even if you want it now, without complaining.

- Resourcefulness – the ability to find a way to accomplish things, even when the answers aren't obvious.

- Sincerity – you really mean what you say; you are genuine, real without ulterior motives.

- Tolerance – ability to accept things, values, and beliefs that are different from your own.

- Virtue – having moral and ethical values and behavior.

- Wisdom – having sound judgment; always open to learning.

How Do You Develop Character?

Your character relates to your personality, but it is not the same thing. Personality comes partially from inborn traits. Your character comes from those around you and your observation of the behaviors of others. You learn values and attitudes from your parents, your teachers or other leaders, and from your friends.

When you review the previous list of words describing character, you will note they are all action words. Your values, beliefs, thoughts and words all become your character when you put them into action. The results are visible. It is not what someone thinks about you, it is what they see you do. Tom Landry, Football Hall of Fame and former Green Bay Packer Coach, said, given the choice between a player with average skills and outstanding character and a player with outstanding skills, he would take the average player every time. His reasoning was that the underlying success factor of good character in everyone would make the average player perform to his fullest potential, while the outstanding player without good character will usually fail to play to their potential, and will often fail to have even an average performance.

"Character is made in the small moments of our lives." —Phillips Brooks

There are several choices you can make as you develop your character. Here are some of the more important ones:

1. Be honest with yourself and others around you. Make sound decisions. Feel good about yourself. Be proud of who you are and what you stand for.

2. Always do your very best, even when it is difficult.

3. Choose to be positive, finding what is good and right in yourself and in others. Have a sense of humor; be able to laugh at yourself.

4. Take responsibility for your thoughts, your words, your choices and your actions. Be responsible for your own mistakes and learn from them. You are responsible for finding your own happiness and reaching your goals.

5. Treat others with honor and respect. Treat them as you would like to be treated.

6. Have tolerance and understanding for the differences in others regardless of race, religion, gender, age, economic status or culture.

7. Always be grateful for what you have, rather than complaining about what you do not have.

8. Be of service to others. Be willing to help others in your family, school, and your community. *You always help yourself when you help others*—American proverb

9. Think about who you want to be, your rules for living, and your goals for the future.

10. Live each moment of your life as if someone is watching you.

Positive vs. Negative

Because your character comes from your attitude, it may be negative or positive or somewhere in-between, depending upon a given situation. The challenges you face that define your character may be a minor issue or a life-changing situation. An example would be, in the face of danger, whether an individual reacts with **courage** (positive) or with **cowardice** (negative). At the same time, a Macho characteristic could be a negative with an exaggerated sense of toughness, and could cause someone to act foolishly in a dangerous situation.

In the effort put forth to complete a task, the positive trait would be "hardworking" and the negative "lazy." See if you can name the negative trait relating to the following positive ones.

1. Confident   _____
2. Conscientious   _____
3. Considerate   _____
4. Determined   _____
5. Fair   _____
6. Generous   _____
7. Honest   _____
8. Kind   _____
9. Polite   _____
10. Reliable   _____

(Answers are at the end of the chapter).

The Importance of Character

Know that the image you have of yourself tomorrow will be based upon the actions you take today. You may be able to hide your thoughts from others, but you will never be able to conceal them from yourself. Will you be proud of the actions you take today?

The confidence you develop comes from how you perceive yourself and how you feel about what you have done. Sometimes you will have to make choices that may be unpopular. Always consider that being popular involves **how others look at you** and not how you see yourself. The choices you make help determine what will happen next. Good character is the single most important underlying factor to success in life. Each of you has the ability to develop, strengthen and even change your character. What you do and how you behave does matter. Having good character makes you a better person, it can make a difference, and it will make your world a better place.

The Person Down the Road

In thirty, forty or fifty years you'll meet a person down the road. Whether that person is kind, gentle, or selfish and demanding depends on what you do today. If you live in terms of what you can get out of life, this person will be crabby, self-centered, and spiteful. But, if you open your life to others and live as a giver, this person will be kind, open and generous. This somebody whom you'll meet down the road someday is you. The person you will be tomorrow depends on the life you live today. Everyday, in every way, you are becoming more and more like yourself. Make sure the person you are becoming is someone you'll enjoy being around.
—Unknown

Answers to Positive vs Negative:
1. Unsure
2. Careless
3. Inconsiderate

4. Indecisive
5. Biased
6. Stingy
7. Dishonest
8. Cruel
9. Rude
10. Unreliable

ABOUT THE AUTHOR

MARILYN STEWART MILLER

Myralyn Stewart Miller, CEO and President of the Stewart Miller Communication Institute for Excellence, Inc., is a speech pathologist, educator and entrepreneur. Myralyn Miller received a Bachelor of Arts Degree in French Liberal Arts and a Master of Arts degree in Speech Pathology with a minor in Linguistics. Extensive studies were in the areas of supervision, administration, leadership, speech pathology and accent reduction.

Myralyn Miller is a ASHA certified and licensed speech pathologist who works extensively with children, youths and adults addressing communication disorders and dysphagia. She has conducted numerous workshops and in-services for parents, staff, peers, educators and administrators relative to speech and language development, vocal abuse behaviors, accent reduction programs and swallowing issues.

As an entrepreneur, Myralyn Miller offered continuing eduction programs as a Florida provider for healthcare professionals. In her free time, she develops speech therapy games, activities and products. She will offer intensive camp programs focusing on "Fast ForWord," social interactions, etiquette skills, speech improvement, language learning and accent enhancement. Myralyn served as board advisor for the Port Gibson Mental Health Center in Mississippi and is a International Advisory Board Member of the Professional Woman Network.

Contact:
Myralyn Miller, MA, CCC-SLP
Stewart Miller Communication Institute for Excellence, Inc.
410-09 Blanding Blvd. #221
Orange Park, FL 32073
(904) 537-3629
myralyn@stewartmillercommunication.com
www.stewartmillercommunication.com

FIVE

COMMUNICATE WITH EASE

By Myralyn Miller

Many research studies have been conducted about communication skills and the perceptions that impact hiring practices, relationships, and leadership potential. This information seemed relevant not only for recruiters who make appropriate candidate selections, but for companies who hire and/or offer communication training programs. Additionally, the information seemed helpful for individuals who want a competitive edge in their quest for personal, academic, vocational, social and professional goals.

Assumptions regarding the reasons for this information may include the following:

• Jobs are not filled with qualified candidates.

• Qualified candidates are not being hired.

• Qualified candidates are not being granted promotions.

- Students are not completing their educational programs.

- Students are not earning grades they deserve.

- Communication is ineffective.

- Communication is inappropriate.

In an independent and random study conducted by Stewart Miller Institute for Excellence, Inc., results indicated that 73% of healthcare visitors and 67% of speech pathologists felt that young men have poor social, listening, vocabulary, conversational and problem-solving skills, and that those skills need to be addressed in order for them to achieve personal, business, social and vocational success. This chapter offers tips, suggestions, techniques and exercises for young men to review and practice throughout the day. The exercises are easy to follow and implement in your daily routine. Each task may be repeated to reflect the changes in your perspectives or your skill level. Maintaining a task journal is suggested for you to review or compare your responses over time. As a dynamic communicator, change is expected as you become more observant of different communication styles, speaking skills and word usage. Let this chapter be a springboard for continuous improvement opportunities on your own, or through the assistance of a speech pathologist or an interpersonal skills trainer.

Listening

Often, many think that listening is just about hearing. During a communication exchange, several interpretations are possible to the question, "Are you hearing me?" Consider the following:

- The person has a hearing loss.

- The person is following oral directions incorrectly.

- The person's behavior is unchanged.

- The person does not seem to grasp the information.

Is it possible that listening ability and skill can be in question during a communication exchange? Absolutely! At some point, no matter what is said or how it is said, difficulty getting the point or following directions can occur. Making sure the information is conveyed as intended and received accurately can be a challenge. Listening is a skill that involves all senses, which requires some engagement and some interpretation in the quest for understanding. Above all, the speaker requires some form of acknowledgement. Mastering listening is the key to success with family, peers, friends, co-workers and your boss.

Listening Assessment: Put an X in the box next to each statement below that characterizes your listening behaviors. This is your honest assessment of your listening skills.

- ❏ I do not interrupt the speaker.

- ❏ I do not show impatience.

- ❏ I do not suggest solutions before hearing the problem completely.

- ❏ I get the message straight.

- ❏ I listen more than I talk.

- ❏ I listen attentively to the speaker without wandering thoughts.

❑   I paraphrase what the speaker is saying.

❑   I summarize the speaker's point before I give my viewpoint.

❑   I defer the discussion until I can give my undivided attention.

❑   I ask open-ended questions to elicit the speaker's thoughts, opinions and feelings.

Listening Skills Improvement Activity: List each listening behavior that you did not mark in the listening assessment. Then, write three improvement suggestions for each listening behavior. Use the following example as a guide:

Example: I interrupt the speaker.
Improvement Suggestion:
Wait until the speaker finishes his thoughts.
Improvement Suggestion:
Paraphrase the speaker's statements.
Improvement Suggestion:
Ask at least two questions to gain more information.

1. Listening Behavior: _____
    Improvement Suggestions: _____
    Improvement Suggestions: _____
    Improvement Suggestions: _____

2. Listening Behavior: _____
    Improvement Suggestions: _____
    Improvement Suggestions: _____

Improvement Suggestions: _____

3. Listening Behavior: _____
    Improvement Suggestions: _____
    Improvement Suggestions: _____
    Improvement Suggestions: _____

Non-Verbal Communication

What is non-verbal communication and how does it impact the message? Nonverbal communication involves body posture, gestures, facial expressions, eye contact and proximity. How you stand or sit may have a bearing on whether someone thinks they can approach you or not. Gestures are movements that can add emphasis to discussions or conversation, and enhance the message, if used judiciously. Facial expressions can convey mood, agreement, and/or friendliness. The appropriate amount of eye contact impacts relationships, perceived interests, and your credibility as a speaker because of the connection you create. Proximity is the amount of distance from the other person, and is usually determined by the relationship established with that individual.

Task: To get a handle on your non-verbal skills, practice speaking words, phrases and sentences in front of a mirror. Speak like you normally speak; but take note of your eye movements, hand gestures and other non-verbal communication skills. How effective are they? Are they used appropriately? Place an **X** in the box under Yes or No to indicate your response to each question.

Listen to the feedback from others about your non-verbal behaviors during and/or after a conversational exchange. Make two copies of this form and label one 'My Impressions' and the other form 'Others' Feedback'. Compare the two.

	YES	NO
Body Posture:		
Do you stand erect?		
Do you sit erect?		
Do you slouch?		
Do you lean in?		
Do you lean back?		
Do you fold your arms?		
Gestures:		
Do your arms flail when you talk?		
Are your gestures timed with your message?		
Are your gestures congruent with your message?		
Do you use head nods efficiently?		
Facial Expressions:		
Do you frown?		
Do you roll your eyes?		
Do you raise your eyebrows?		
Do you smile?		
Eye Contact:		
Do you stare?		

Do your eyes dart back and forth?		
Do you look away?		
Proximity:		
Is your distance in agreement with the social setting?		
Do you get in the person's face?		
Do you touch people during the conversational exchange?		

Meeting People, Making Friends, and Establishing Rapport

How you greet someone, carry yourself, or exchange glances may give a perception about how interesting your conversation may be, and whether someone is willing to spend time talking with you. If you do not look interesting or appear to have something worthwhile to say, your chances of getting to first base or an invitation to the golf course are slim to none. Most people can walk up to someone and say "Hello", but what happens after the "Hello?" The types of questions you ask and the feedback you give are crucial for forming a new friend or gaining a business opportunity.

Task: People Skills Self-Assessment

Put yourself in each situation and answer the questions to gain insight about your people skills.

What do you do or say when you are at a party and the only person you know is the host?

_____

_____

_____

What do you say to someone you have admired from a distance and a chance meeting occurs?

_____

_____

_____

What do you say to a stranger on a plane?

_____

_____

_____

Sample study suggestions below provide a starting point for developing small talk skills. The key is having a repertoire of information about various topics, current events, occupations, hobbies, etc. The skill you want is the ability to provide a turn taking information or to ask questions that will elicit information from others, while you come across as being not only knowledgeable, but interested in them.

1. Practice asking open-ended questions that start or continue a conversation.

2. Become familiar with information and key words unique to different professions, hobbies and sports.

3. Learn about pets.

Task A: Research the following occupations. This is an information-gathering task for small talk. Complete the exercise following the Speech Therapy Example.

Subject	Unique Words	Info/ Description	Question to Ask
Speech Therapy	Articulation, Dysphagia	Communication, Swallowing Problems	Where do you practice? What is your expertise?
Web Designer			
Anthropologist			

Task B: Research high profile people. This is an information-gathering task for small talk. Complete the exercise following the Tiger Woods example.

Subject	Unique Words	Info/ Description	Questions
Tiger Woods	Putt, 9 Iron, PGA, Hole-in-one	Professional Golfer Recently married	How did you get interested in golf?
Tavis Smiley			
Oprah Winfrey			

Task C: List subjects, hobbies, occupations and/or people that interest you. This is your information gathering for small talk. Complete the task on your own or with a partner.

Subject	Unique Words	Info/ Descriptions	Questions

Communication Barriers

Any physical or psychological feature can impact message reception and understanding by stopping, interrupting, or filtering the flow of information. These are distractions, and the reactions to them can significantly reduce meaningful dialogue. Knowing yourself in the role of speaker or listener can prepare you for managing these barriers and/or lessening their impact on communication.

Assessment Exercise: Review the list of filters or barriers that follow. Brief descriptions and/or examples are presented to clarify each barrier type for your reference point. Be honest. This is about you. This is self-revealing information to gain insight into your communication style. As you read each one, ask yourself one or more of these questions. "Could I become distracted by…?" "Will my reaction to this distraction prevent meaningful dialogue?" "Do I wander off during a lecture or instruction?" "Do I let my personal feelings or beliefs keep me from listening effectively, or learning from an opportunity?" Place a check mark by the ones that received at least one "Yes" response.

❏ **Bias** - Personal beliefs or opinions based on your background, culture, past experiences

❏ **Attention** - Any internal or external distraction, i.e., boring topic, headache, test results

❏ **Environmental** - Temperature, lighting, cluttered room, seating capacity or comfort

❑ **Noise** - Any distracting sound, i.e., lawnmower, traffic, coughing, ringing phone

❑ **Stress** - Any personal or business pressures, i.e., health issues, tests, deadlines

❑ **Culture** - Upbringing, mores, traditions

❑ **Values** - Views on right or wrong, good or bad in every aspect of life

❑ **Gender** - Differences in male and female communication styles, reactions

❑ **Age** - Vocabulary, language use, experiences, knowledge

❑ **Education** - Degree advancement, literary experiences, subject knowledge

❑ **Listening Flaws** - Giving advice, defensiveness, one-upmanship, telling others how to feel

Barrier Solution Activity: Follow the example below to address the top three barriers/filters you checked in the Barrier Assessment Exercise. Team up with a partner and brainstorm suggestions and possible solutions that can help you implement them efficiently and with ease to reduce the impact of those barriers or distractions during your communication interactions.

Barrier Example: Environmental (The room is too cold)

Put on a coat. Turn up the thermostat. Invite the person or parties involved to a warmer location. You may say, "I have really been looking forward to hearing what you have to suggest. Let's get closer to the fireplace."

Barrier #1 _____

_____

_____

Barrier #2 _____

_____

_____

Barrier #3 _____

_____

_____

Tips for Your Communication Journey

1. Speak without using vocal intrusions, such as "ahm", "ah", "okay", "you know".

2. Stand erect at the lectern making sure the microphone is positioned at a comfortable height for speaking without leaning into the microphone.

3. Keep your fingers still. Do not tap the podium.

4. Create a relaxed face. Smile. Do not frown.

5. Use accurate pronunciation skills.

6. Construct grammatically accurate sentences.

7. Expand your vocabulary by reading or listening to others.

8. Use air for speaking efficiently with appropriate pause breaks.

Communication Accountability

Communication presumes truth. What you say and how you say it impacts your relationships with clients, peers, staff, administrators, healthcare providers, family members and friends. The degree of information you share depends on your purpose and the person with whom you are talking. Having knowledge is important; but conveying that knowledge to inform or persuade by using tact, showing confidence, and displaying credibility is compelling. Giving instructions, making announcements, creating emails or writing memos are ways of sending information. Information and communication are different. Both, in concert, can be very powerful. How you are perceived impacts your effectiveness. When you know the message you want to convey and you know how you want the listener to feel, then you can work on creating a message that inspires a positive action by getting people to develop a personal connection with you. When this occurs, communication becomes a vehicle that inspires action, rather than just transferring information.

1. If your listeners are moved to action, your communication is effective.

2. If your listeners are able to follow and comprehend your message, your communication is effective.

3. If your listeners grasp your message and your priorities are clearly understood, your communication is effective.

4. If your listeners are captivated by your message, your communication is effective.

Therefore, strive to be an effective communicator and make a commitment to have successful relationships, interviews, academic outcomes, leadership skills, and career moves. The door is open for your steps to communication accountability and unbelievable rewards.

ABOUT THE AUTHOR

GLENDA Y. HICKS

Glenda Y. Hicks is a Certified Public Accountant, licensed in the states of Georgia and Florida. She holds a Bachelor of Science degree in Accounting from Florida State University and a Master of Professional Accounting degree from the University of Miami. She has 20 years of experience in the profession and owns her own CPA firm in Marietta, Georgia. Mrs. Hicks serves the nonprofit community, by providing a myriad of consulting services in the area of financial management and tax research, in a capacity as CFO by the Hour as well as on a project basis.

Mrs. Hicks is a member of the Professional Woman Network, an international training organization, and is trained in offering workshops focused on women's issues such as Managing Stress, the Superwoman Syndrome, and Building Positive Self Esteem. She is co-author of the recently released book, "Women's Journey to Wellness: Mind, Body, and Spirit" and will co-author two additional books, "Emotional Wellness for Women Volumes I and II within the next year. Mrs. Hicks has served as a volunteer group facilitator for women of domestic violence, in the areas of self esteem and managing stress for the YWCA of Northwest Georgia. She is active in her community and is the immediate past Treasurer for Girls on the Run of Atlanta, Inc., a nonprofit organization that seeks to educate and prepare girls for a lifetime of self respect and healthy living through training them to run a 5K race.

Audiences for Mrs. Hicks' presentations have included such organizations as the National Association of Black Accountants, the Atlanta Women's Alliance, the Pfizer Foundation, Kennesaw State University, and the Georgia Low Voltage Contractors.

Contact:
Glenda Y. Hicks, CPA
1750 Powder Springs Road
Suite 190, PMB 267
Marietta, GA 30064
770-423-7113 phone
glenda@gyhickscpa.com
www.gyhickscpa.com

SIX

CHOICES: TAKING RESPONSIBILITY

By Glenda Hicks

The Spirit of the Sovereign Lord is upon me,
Because the Lord has anointed me to preach good news to the poor.
He has sent me to bind up the brokenhearted,
Proclaim freedom for the captives,
And release from darkness for the prisoners.
—Isaiah 61:1

We all have a purpose in this life, and it is more than being born, living, and then dying. As part of the big picture, we are to bind up (or lift up) the brokenhearted, proclaim freedom (or victory) for those who are living in captivity to whatever issues are holding them down (or back), and release from the darkness of ignorance, confusion, and misdirection those who are prisoners in their own lives.

When I was invited to participate in this book, I reflected on the lives of the men in my life. I thought about my father (who is now deceased), my brother, my husband, and our son, as well as the extended men in my life, such as my uncles, nephews, brothers-in-law, and male cousins. Given my observations, experiences, and responsibilities with these men, I was compelled to accept the invitation so that I could impart some of what I have come to learn and believe are critical considerations for a young man's success.

In the opening scripture, poor does not mean monetary wealth. It refers to those who are "lacking". For young men who may be lacking in areas such as relationships (with friends, family, women, and/or work), decision-making skills, leadership, finances, success, health, career, spirituality, joy, peace, and more, I submit to you that your choices (and taking responsibility for those choices) have a lot to do with every aspect of your life.

I hope this chapter will resonate with you, cause you to examine your life and your choices, and will help you discover who you really are, what the plan is for your life, and what choices you need to make to transform into the person God has ordained you to be, and not what "man" says you should be.

How Are You Being Raised?

You are a product of many things. At this point in your life, you have become who you are because of the places you have lived while growing up, and the people who have been around you during those years. The outcome also depends upon whether you are being raised by your mother, father, (or both), or perhaps a grandparent, aunt or uncle; receiving a good education or not; attending or plan to attend college; planning to join the military and why; growing up in the inner city or suburbs, a big city, or small town; have a lot of friends or a few; attend church, have a close relationship with your immediate family; know your birth parents; whether you are adopted, and so much more.

Exercise #1

Have you ever stopped to think about these questions? If not, take some time and do it now. What is so remarkable about this process is that it helps you to review the choices you made or did not make, as well as those choices that were made or not made by others in your life which have led to the shaping of who you are and where you are right now. The good news here is that you do not have to live with what you discover. You can use the information to accept the past for what it is, and then make new choices to change your reality, if that is what you need and desire. You are the master of your fate. God has the plan, but you have to make the choices to fulfill that plan.

Write a paragraph about how you grew up, with whom, where, and the impact of the environment and family on your life and your choices:

_____

_____

_____

_____

_____

_____

(Use extra paper to share your thoughts)

Are You Angry?

Do you blame someone else for your current situation? So many young men do. Maybe you blame your father for leaving you and your mother. Perhaps you blame your parents for not providing a better life growing up. Maybe you make excuses for not having enough money to further your education because of the actions (or inaction) of someone else. Did you get involved with a girl and now you have a child earlier than you planned? Were you abused as a child? Each of these situations (and countless more that I did not list) involves another person whom I am sure you can very easily blame for why you feel cheated. It may be true that others share in the blame and responsibility to some degree for who and where you are, but that fact does not have to keep you from where you are going!

Exercise #2
Make a list of the areas in your life for which you blame someone else for your current situation. This can be very painful, so take your time and be honest.

CURRENT SITUATION	THE PERSON YOU BLAME	WHAT THEY KEPT YOU FROM ACHIEVING

Okay, obstacles have been in your way and prevented you from achieving. Now, what are you going to do to achieve these goals and dreams? For these items, identify what steps you need to take to achieve them. Do you need money, skills, or education? Whatever it is that you need, create a plan for how you will do it. Enumerate the specific steps you need to take, identify the people you need to involve in the process (perhaps not by name, but by function/skill), and set target dates for achieving each step. If you need help in sorting your plan, seek input from a trusted friend or adult. Now, GO!

For the people on your list who "prevented" you from achieving your goals…..forgive them. You do not have to go to them and forgive them in person; just forgive them in your heart. What so many young men fail to realize is that no one is perfect, and everybody makes mistakes. The people you blame may have been ill equipped to lead you properly. Others may have been too immature to have given you guidance. Still others may have been angry and frustrated themselves, and therefore incapable or unwilling to be a beacon of light for you. And of course, there is envy. Many people will not do for others because they do not want them to experience a better life than their own (many "friends" fit into this category). Let the anger go because it is doing nothing but crippling you. Consider that the very person you are blaming is probably oblivious to what they have done to you (or not done for you); and while they are proceeding with their own lives, you are reliving the "what could have beens" and harboring anger which is holding you back, preventing you from making the moves you need to make, and simply getting you nowhere, fast.

The Company You Keep: Guilt By Association

Who is a part of your circle? Who do you hang around with? Are they young men on the fringes of crime, or young scholars or athletes on the road to productive lives? Do you mingle with students who plan to attend college, join the military, or seek a job to support themselves and lead them to greater heights? Are you surrounding yourself with adults who can help you prepare for a career, give you advice on financing your college education, or successful male mentors who can help you sort through difficult issues?

Do you understand the significance of the company you keep? So many young men find themselves in questionable situations when they are young because they do not know any better. Or perhaps they know better, but do not think they will get caught. Maybe they do not care. Maybe they think the situation is just fun and games. What are you doing with your time?

I will never forget how my brother always felt my father was harder on him than he was on my sister and me. My brother always seemed to be disciplined more often or more harshly than we were. In hindsight, he was, and with good reason. Our parents knew (and in particular, my father knew) that they had to raise a boy into a man that would respect his own life, respect the lives of others, respect women, and be a responsible father for his own family one day while contributing to society. Our parents made sure they knew all our friends, and knew where we were at all times. They knew what time we were leaving, where we were going, who was going to be there, and what time we were expected home. So many times we did not understand (or at least I did not understand) the rules. But now we do. My brother is alive; he is married with five children, is a successful attorney, a loving father, husband, son, brother, friend, and is a man of God.

But this path is no guarantee. Why? Because you, as the individual, make the choices and take the responsibility for your own life. Your parents may set the rules, but do you follow them? Many young men have had similar childhoods as my brother, but now they are dead or in jail. Why is that? I submit to you that it is the choices they made. Where do you want to be? What choices will you make?

My husband and I raise our kids together. But he has already told me that when it comes to our son, there will be times when I will need to stay out of the matter and let him handle things. I fully understand what he means and why; and have committed that I will comply.

Man Up!

I am sure you have heard this phrase "Man Up!" Was it said to you? Have you said it to your brother, your cousin, a teammate, an opponent, or maybe you just heard it in a movie or television show. What does this say to you? Does it say, "Move on?" Does it say, "Take responsibility?" Does it say, "It is up to me?" Does it say, "I can do all things through Christ who strengthens me?" Does it say, "Maybe it was my fault. I'm sorry?" Most often, when I hear "Man Up!" it refers to acting like a man is "supposed" to act, such as not crying when he gets injured in a sporting event (i.e. Little League). "Man Up" should mean so much more than this. It should mean making the difficult and perhaps time consuming choices that force you to take responsibility for your life and your circumstances. The road less traveled is less traveled for a reason—it is usually more difficult. The rewards, however, are so much sweeter—peace, joy, and success. You were never promised an easy life, but you were promised that you would be equipped to handle whatever comes your way. Your burdens will never be more than you can ultimately bear, and in every trial there is a lesson. Start paying attention and learn from them. Until you learn the lesson, you will continue to repeat the test. Therefore, understand that "Man Up" really should mean taking responsibility for yourself, your actions, and your choices.

Reality Check

Right about now you are probably thinking, "All of this sounds great, but you do not know my situation because......." You can fill in the blank with whatever makes it fit your situation. For example, "Because I've been in jail and no one will hire me", or "Because I live in a drug and crime ridden inner-city, and no one gets out of here", or "Because my father left our family, and I have to help my mom run the household." Well, you are correct! I do not know. But I do know that God created you and has a plan for you. He gave you free will, and you can make choices. How hungry are you? How badly do you want change? How tired are you with your current situation? Know that you are not alone, and you are not the only young man facing what you are facing. Your success depends upon your choices. Seek out people, information, books, mentors, places, careers, guidance, and whatever else you need from sources that can identify and relate to your circumstances. Rarely will you encounter a situation that someone else has not already encountered and overcome themselves.

You are living in the best of times this world has ever known when it comes to opportunity. Whatever you once dreamed for yourself can still be achieved, but you have to be willing to make the right choices, take responsibility for your actions, and never give up. You will indeed face difficult times, unfair decisions made against you, people who will try to pull you down and say you will never amount to anything, but those are people who are bitter and envy the opportunity that they see you have available to you. I know this is true because there are men in my life who have lived this story. They have overcome the odds because they refused to accept what someone else wanted to define for their lives.

Role Models

Exercise #3

Who are your role models? Why? Take a moment to complete the table below.

ROLE MODEL (NAME)	WHY? (REASON FOR YOUR CHOICE)

Many young teens list professional athletes as their role models. I suspect you have a few on your list, too. Is it because of their fame and fortune, or because of their character? Unfortunately, many athletes have fallen from grace in recent years, and corporate leaders are no exception. So, what is the answer in choosing your role models? As much as it is possible, look at the character of the person. Character will outlive fame and fortune every time. It is certainly inspiring to choose famous people and aspire to what they have achieved. In your everyday life, however, be sure to choose a few role models who you either know personally and can access as mentors, or who are leaders in your community that you can realistically access by way of school assignments or school athletics. This will position people in your circle who can directly impact your life and expose you to opportunities you may not otherwise encounter. Now, re-evaluate your list above, and see if you want to make any changes.

Preparation + Opportunity = Success

When opportunity knocks, will you be prepared? As a young teen, now is the time to begin laying the foundation for your success. What organizations are you involved in at your school? I speak to and interact with high school students and teachers, college students and professors, and corporate professionals on a regular basis. What I have repeatedly seen and heard is that individuals who are offered the best (and most) opportunities are those who can present themselves well, speak with confidence, have work experience (paid or in a volunteer capacity), have solid oral and written communication skills, work well on a team, can think and analyze a situation, and know how to prepare a resume and use basic computer programs (e.g. Microsoft Word, Microsoft EXCEL). You can gain these skills right now as a teen if you choose to do so. Your school is replete with clubs, competitions, counselors, teachers, and sports teams that can teach you all these skills. Join a club. Get involved in a sport, serve on a committee, or run for an office. The resources are there for you. Take advantage of them! When opportunity passes your way, you may only have that one chance to pursue it. Make sure you are prepared.

Helpful Tool

Use the following table to identify which responsibilities and roles are applicable to your life. What choices will you make concerning them?

RESPONSIBILITY	CHOICE
College	
Being a Father	
Athlete	
Son	
Employee	
Brother	

Mentor	
Student	
Friend	
Church Member	
Community Volunteer	
Tough Guy	
Fearless	
"The Man"	
Humble Servant	
Visionary/Dreamer	
Primary Wage Earner	

Challenge

I challenge you to take an account of your life and determine where you are headed. Assess the choices you have made, as well as those that have been made for you, and decide where you need to go from here. As you order your life and pursue your goals, remember your responsibility to serve someone else. Reach back. Help another young man find his way. Do not sit on the sidelines of life and watch the game. Get in the game and make the plays yourself!

Recommended Reading

Seek books, tapes, and magazines that add value to your life. Learn from your mistakes, as well as the mistakes of others. Design the life you live by the choices you make. Take the choices that have been made for you (for which you had no control), re-work them, and move on.

Do It Afraid by Joyce Meyer

Rescued by John Bevere

Gifted Hands: The Ben Carson Story by Ben Carson

Live Your Dreams by Les Brown

Black Enterprise Magazine

Notes:

_____

_____

_____

_____

_____

_____

_____

_____

_____

_____

_____

_____

_____

_____

_____

_____

_____

_____

_____

_____

_____

ABOUT THE AUTHOR

Iva Sherrill-Edwards

Ms. Iva Sherrill-Edwards is a Forensic Document Examiner, specializing in Handwriting Identification and Signature Verification. She was born in Little Rock, Arkansas, and was raise up in Cincinnati, Ohio. She has lived in Phoenix and Scottsdale, Arizona for Twelve years, and recently relocated back to Cincinnati, Ohio.

Ms. Iva Sherrill-Edwards earned a Bachelors of Science degree in Business Administration from The Union Institute University, Cincinnati, Ohio.

She has been a workshop trainer for youth, and conducts workshops for at-risk teen boys at a Charter school in Cincinnati, Ohio, specializing in presenting Personal Development and Life Skills training. She was the President of Success Images Unlimited, A Professional Development and Management Consulting firm in Cincinnati, Ohio and has experience as a classroom teacher and Certified Handwriting Analyst.

Ms. Iva Sherrill-Edwards is a certified trainer with The Professional Woman Network, an international consulting organization specializing in personal and professional development for women. She is available to assist attorneys and their clients with Handwriting Identification, Contested Wills and Contract documents, and is available to present speeches on Forensic Document Examination methods and tools to groups.

Ms. Iva Sherrill-Edwards is available for group presentation (professional, government and students), and conducts workshops and seminars throughout the United States. She is a member of The Professional Woman Network International Advisory Board and The Association of Document Examiners.

Contact:
Ms. Iva Sherrill-Edwards
P.O. Box 37197
Cincinnati, Ohio 45222
Phone/Fax: 513-662-0064
Email: FDE1edwards@aol.com
www.ohiodocumentexaminer.com

SEVEN

20 STEPS FOR BUILDING SELF-WORTH

By Iva Sherrill-Edwards

If you are to develop self-worth, you must become empowered. Self-empowerment means to take control and be in charge of your life as you develop self-worth. I would like to offer you 20 Steps for Building Self-Worth that will last you a lifetime.

1. The first step is to **always believe in yourself,** even when others don't. Reflect on what makes you unique and different from others. 'I believe in me' is the confidence to make plans for your life with the hope and understanding that you will succeed in your plans.

    *   Have a passion for your life plans and have passion to live life with joy and happiness.

    *   Take pride in what makes you unique.

- Learn how to love yourself above all else and understand that you are of value to yourself and others.

2. **Develop a positive attitude** towards life. Your attitude is a priceless possession, and you should treasure it. Your attitude will determine your success and reward in life. It will determine how much success you achieve in life. Remember, your thoughts are words (negative or positive) spoken within your mind. Your thoughts must have a vision, which shows you and others that something good is happening in your life. When something good is happening in your life, family and friends will encourage you to continue to reach for greater success. Watch your thoughts. Don't let negative thoughts begin in your mind. Your mind controls your attitude. What you can believe, you can achieve with a positive mental attitude!

   "Motivation, Education and Determination = A Successful Positive Attitude—Your Most Priceless Possession."

3. **Perform to the best of your ability** in whatever you endeavor to accomplish. Look at yourself and be real about what you want to accomplish. Look at yourself and decide what strategy you will use to accomplish your goals. You are a leader of your life, and the first law of leadership 'is to truly believe in your message (plans for your life) and others will believe in you, the messenger'. Know your limitations and what your strengths and weaknesses are.

   Make a list of what you consider your strengths and weaknesses.

	Strengths	Weaknesses

4. **Holding yourself in high esteem** means to feel good about yourself and your abilities, praising yourself on your past accomplishments, and not dwelling on your past mistakes. Remember, your past life doesn't have to determine your future life. Decide that you are going to be successful in life, make an action plan, and stick to it as you take positive steps toward a more successful future.

5. **Have confidence in your ability** to make changes and meet life's challenges head-on. Think for yourself; trust your own judgment, and learn to make your own decisions with proper guidance. Learn to trust your decision-making ability, but know there may be times you will make unwise decisions. Do seek advice from your parents, mentor, or other members of your support system that will help you make wise choices.

6. **Have a support system or mentor** that will always be available to listen and help you make wise decisions and choices, and help guide you on the right path. (You may not have family members or friends who support you in whatever path you choose to follow, so don't let *negative* friends and family members direct your life with their words or thoughts.) Choose positive people and good role models to mentor you and offer guidance. Drop them a card of thanks, phone call, or email them and let them know how much they mean in your life.

7. **Avoid comparing yourself to others.** Expect the best of yourself at all times. Constantly seek ways to improve your environment and yourself. Remember, you cannot change what you do not acknowledge. If you need help of any kind, don't be afraid to ask for it. By denying your problems, you deny yourself the chance of finding a solution, and that will assure your success.

8. **Constantly seek ways to improve yourself.** Take action to accomplish some goal each day so that you don't miss your window of opportunity. **Action + Preparation = Success!** Don't give up if you don't succeed immediately at something. Quitters never win, and Winners never quit! Consider ways you might begin to improve yourself, including how you dress, talk, whether your hand shake is firm, and if you look a person in the eye when you are talking to them.

9. **Set goals that are realistic and achievable.**

   • Set short and long-term goals. (Short-term goals should be something you can accomplish between six months to a year; long-term is between five and ten years.)

- Set lifetime goals (what you want to achieve by certain milestones in your life).

- List dreams you want to achieve.

Long-Term Goals:

Short-Term Goals:

Lifetime Goals:

Dreams You Want To Achieve:

- Once you have achieved a goal, celebrate and reward yourself. Cross it off your list and move on to the next goal. Say to yourself, "What can I do today to help me reach my next goal?"

10. **As you strive towards excellence** and plan your future, *act like a winner*. Associate with successful people you admire and from whom you can learn life lessons. Let them be your role models.

List the people in your life whom you admire and can learn from their lessons:

What special gifts do these role models possess?

11. **Visualize your future.** Create a clear picture in your mind of what you want to accomplish in your lifetime. (Picture yourself graduating from high school, graduating from college with an associate degree, bachelor degree or Masters Degree.) Remember, an artist can only paint a picture after they have received a vision to paint. What type of artist are you? The purpose of this step is

to take your dreams or goals and turn them into reality. There is a saying that you should write down the vision of the life that you want and visualize it. But do start by creating a mental image of something you plan to acquire or do in the future. The clearer the image, the stronger the belief in your vision, and the more likely that you will take action to accomplish that belief.

12. **Accept who you are,** and have the courage and strength to design your life the way **you** want it to be. According to Danny Kaye, *"Life is a great big canvas, and you should throw all the paint on it you can."*

Write about an adventure or experience you would like to have in your lifetime.

13. **Develop and maintain your credibility.** Your success will be a direct result of your integrity. "To thine own self be true." Remember, your reputation is all you really have, and you want others to know you are honest and a person of your word.

- Let your actions speak of your values and be an indication of your character as a person and human being in this world.

- Think of your reputation and your spoken words as pure gold.

- Honesty + Integrity = Reputation.

14. **Acknowledge that there is a force in the universe** greater than yourself (whatever you believe), and that it will always be there for you. There is an inner spirit within all of us, and you need to listen so you can hear the inner voice speaking to you. Maintain a calm mind and be at peace with yourself and all that is around you. Think about what a miracle your life is now, and the blessings you have received. The divine spirit within you is available to guide, heal, and prosper you if you believe. Enjoy your life and live it with passion in all you do. Ben Sira writes, "Happy the man who mediates on wisdom, reflects on knowledge, nourishes himself on the bread of understanding, and is given the water of learning to drink."

15. **Define Success**

    Success to me is:

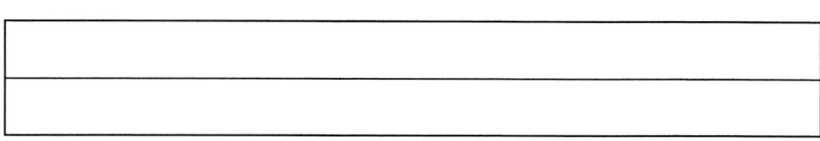

16. **Whose goals are they?** As you take one step at a time toward your goals, you will be surprised how many people come into your life to help you achieve them. Make sure your goals are the ones you want to accomplish for yourself, not the ones your parents or friends want for you. If you try to pursue a goal or dream for someone else, you will never be happy. Just remember, family and friends should support you in your dream to achieve whatever you desire.

To help you set your goals:

- Develop an action plan.

- Set a time limit on when you want to accomplish a goal.

- Decide on how you will attain the skills needed to succeed with your plan.

- Get your support system in place.

- Ask your parent, a mentor, or someone you admire to help guide you.

17. **Time management** is an important part of growing up and setting goals. You have to be able to manage your time effectively to succeed. Some techniques to stay focused with your time management are:

- Buy a notebook or journal to keep a schedule.

- Outline a schedule of all your activity/classes/work.

- Schedule from Monday through Friday all the things you have to do.

- Place a time limit on accomplishing or completing each task/activity.

- Schedule time for reading, prayer and relaxation.

Planning is the key to staying focused on what you want to accomplish in the time allotted. The intelligent use of your time leads to more successes.

18. **Recognize your own leadership qualities. What are they?**

| |
| |
| |
| |
| |
| |
| |

Some leadership qualities to consider:

- **Determination.** Be determined to stay focused on your goals.

- **Passion.** Be passionate about whatever you decide will be your life's work.

- **Results oriented.** Leaders like to see results from their efforts.

- **Visionary.** Do you see yourself changing life for others or improving the world?

- **Charisma.** A charismatic person is charming with a magnetic personality.

19. **Be a life-long learner.** There is always something more to learn. You don't learn everything in school. As a teen, you must read more magazines, books, and your school work, anything that will provide you with knowledge and information that will keep you informed about the world around you.

    - **Keep an open mind.** Don't feel that others can't teach you anything. Sometimes you may even learn from a child.

    - **Network with others.** Don't feel that you can accomplish everything on your own. You can learn from others who have succeeded at one of your goals.

20. **Expect the best of yourself.**

    - **Persevere** - This is the ability to hang in there when all seems lost and you think no one cares.

    - **Use Self-Control** - Make wise decisions; don't take everything personally, as it may not be personal. If you give respect, you will receive respect in return.

    - **Nurture Your Spirit** - Give thanks to some higher power, and walk with your head held high with dignity, confidence and self-awareness. Be committed to your goals and dreams.

Remember: Success is not a destination. It is a journey. Enjoy the ride and have a wonderful life.

I would like to leave you with the following thoughts.

Dream Big Dreams

Allow yourself to dream big dreams. You need hope within yourself to have a dream come true. Dreaming big dreams that are achievable improves your self-confidence, self-respect, your personal happiness, and stimulates you to do better than you have ever done before. **Take the first step toward your dream goal today!**

Reading Resources:

Life Strategies for Teens by Jay McGraw

The 7 Habits of Highly Effective Teens by Sean Covey

Notes:

_____

_____

_____

_____

_____

_____

_____

_____

_____

_____

_____

_____

_____

_____

_____

_____

_____

_____

_____

_____

_____

_____

_____

ABOUT THE AUTHOR

FLORENCE HOPKINS

Florence Hopkins is president and chief executive officer of The Hopkins Consulting Group which specializes in training workshops and empowerment seminars for personal and professional development. She established The Hopkins Consulting Group with a passion for helping individuals and organizations harness their talents and skills to achieve greater personal and professional success. Over the years, she has been a member of a number of organizations that are dedicated to the education and enrichment of women including NAFE, National Association of Business and Professional Women, 100 Black Women, and she is currently a Board member of the Professional Woman Network.

Ms. Hopkins holds a Masters Of Science degree in Telecommunications Policy from The George Washington University in Washington, D.C. Her professional background includes over twenty-five years of experience with AT&T Communications where she held a variety of management positions ranging from operations to product management, marketing and internal auditing. She has parlayed those skills into helping others through motivational speaking and working with individuals and organizations as a Life Coach professional. She is a certified trainer in a number of areas including Women's Issues and Diversity, Leadership and Empowerment skills for Youth, and Branding and Imaging. She is a community leader, mentor and activist in her local community.

Contact:
Florence Hopkins
The Hopkins Consulting Group
Flo1@Comcast.net
(862)452.6303

EIGHT

UNDER FIRE: HANDLING PEER PRESSURE

By Florence Hopkins

What Is Peer Pressure?

Have you ever been pressured into cutting class to hang out with your friends? Has anyone ever said to you, "C'mon, take a hit of this, it won't hurt you!" Did you ever participate in harassing or bullying someone because some of your friends were doing it? If so, then you were a victim of peer pressure. It is defined as the influence your friends and associates have over your beliefs, actions and behavior. Peer pressure has an enormous affect on our entire society, but its greatest impact is on teens and young adults. It influences the styles you wear, your social activities, the friends you select, and many of the daily decisions you make.

As you begin to establish your own independence, peer pressure significantly impacts your social development in terms of the values and principles you set for yourself. It has been a pivotal force in fomenting the change in social mores embraced by teens and young adults today, i.e., dating, sex, alcohol, and drugs.

How strong an influence does peer pressure have on your life? Do you rely on the opinions of your friends to make decisions, or are you comfortable making you own? If your answer is yes, then your friends may have too much influence on you, and this might be a good time to evaluate your self-esteem. Why? Because it may be that you're compromising yourself to gain acceptance from your friends and peers. Soliciting input from friends is not a bad thing, but if you can't make decisions without their opinions, then it could be an indication that you value other people's opinions more than you value yourself.

The downside to this mindset is that you could be more susceptible to the negative influences of peer pressure than you think. Therefore, it is very important that you seek out individuals and activities that will help build your self-confidence and give you a positive self-image. As you begin to move out from the influence of parents and into your own identity, it is crucial that you begin to define who you are, what you believe in, and your goals and aspirations. Doing so will give your life focus and direction, as well as the confidence to make constructive choices and decisions about your life.

Exercise 1:
1. Who are you peers? List some of their names.

_____

_____

_____

2. List a few of your experiences with peer pressure. What influence did your peers have on these experiences?

_____

_____

_____

3. Discuss the importance of self-esteem when dealing with peer pressure.

_____

_____

_____

4. How important are your friends' opinions regarding the choices and decisions you make?

- Important_____
- Somewhat Important_____
- Not Important_____

5. What are some of the risks associated with letting others make decisions and choices for you? What are some of the benefits?

_____

_____

_____

_____

Environmental Influences On Peer Pressure

Depending on your environment and circumstances, the effects of peer pressure can render either positive and/or negative impacts on your life. There are many factors that play a supporting role in determining these effects. The following are representative of just a few:

- A positive, nurturing family is essential in building the character and virtues that are needed to become a productive human being. After all family, in most cases, is the base of your principles, morals and social skills from which you begin to establish your independence and build your own life. Strong family values not only enhance your self-worth, but they can be a deterrent against the influence of negative peer pressure.

• Effective and active community leadership through churches, schools, mentors, and youth groups can provide vital support in the social development of teens and young adults. They can offer surrogate guidance, direction, and motivation outside of the home, in regards to violence prevention, anger management, as well as mediation and tolerance to mitigate the high rate of teen aggression.

• The socio-economic blight in many urban areas is taking an alarming toll on the hopes and dreams of many young male teens. Add to this mix disturbing school dropout rates and high unemployment, and we have a recipe for not only anger and frustration, but also vulnerability to risk factors such as drugs, violent crime, and gang influences.

• New educational and social initiatives are needed badly to ensure that all youth are 1) educated, 2) trained to meet the demands of today's workforce, and 3) given every opportunity to become productive citizens in our society.

Exercise 2:
1. Discuss the role that social circumstances play in effectively handling peer pressure.

_____

_____

_____

2. Identify some of the leaders, mentors and role models in your community that you respect.

_____

_____

_____

3. In what ways do they offer their support and help to build positive self-esteem among the youth in your community? How about your life?

_____

_____

_____

4. In your community, what resources do you feel are needed to help you handle peer pressure more effectively? More parental, school, or police involvement? Other?

_____

_____

_____

Positive Peer Pressure

Peer pressure rooted in positive objectives can be the catalyst to motivate and inspire you to pursue your goals and dreams. As you mature into your own identity, you need to cultivate relationships with people, in your age group, who share your values, opinions, and interests. Friends and associates who are positive, goal-oriented individuals can be great role models and mentors to you. They offer another strata of belonging and acceptance that is needed when you're transitioning into manhood and struggling to find your place in the world. Because they know and understand you, they provide a forum for you to express your views and assert your independence as a young adult. Their insights and feedback could serve as an asset in helping you to prioritize the issues that matter to you in life, i.e. your studies, your grades, and career aspirations.

When dealing with friends, remember that your peers can be your greatest allies or your greatest foes. You need to know the difference! As you build and develop relationships with others, determine whether or not the values and interests of your friends are really in synch with your values. Understanding the dynamics of your friendships will help you to gauge and navigate the choices in friendships that you establish. Staying positive can be a challenge for many young adults, but one way to enhance the power of positive peer influence is to diversify your interests. Having diverse interests will allow you to tap into talents and skills that could open up a variety of opportunities for you. Consider pursuing activities in the arts, e.g. music, acting, karate, sports, or do volunteer work helping other young people. All of these interests build your self-confidence, your knowledge and discipline, as well as expose you to peers who may become a positive influence on you!

Exercise 3:
1. List some of the experiences you've had with positive peer pressure.

_____

_____

_____

2. How have the effects of positive peer pressure benefited your life?

_____

_____

_____

3. What are some of your values and interests?

_____

_____

_____

4. In what ways do your friends and peers show that they value you? Your Interests?

_____

_____

_____

5. Have you ever compromised your values and/or interest to be accepted by friends? If so, explain why?

_____

_____

_____

6. Discuss the problems or conflicts this may have created for you?

_____

_____

_____

7. What activities do you engage in on a regular basis to maintain a positive focus? To meet friends? Discuss how these activities are helping you to build self-esteem and positive relations with other peers?

_____

_____

_____

Negative Peer Pressure

Peer pressure that is misguided and grounded in malicious intentions can produce damaging consequences that resonate well into your adult life. As a society, we are seeing the proliferation of negative peer influence with alarming impacts on our young people. The disturbing rise in crime and handgun use, the abuse of cigarettes, alcohol, drugs, and promiscuous behavior have all culminated into a major social crisis in our society. The compelling force behind this crisis is the intense need to be liked, and to be accepted by our friends and peers. Teens thrive off of this obsession to the point where it has triggered a high degree of conformity to rude, negative, even raunchy behavior patterns. No one wants to stand out from the crowd or be rejected for being 'weird' or 'un-cool.' As a result, many young people are going along with these antics, just to be accepted by friends.

The media has been a big culprit in fueling this behavior with its constant coverage and glamorization of celebrities who have been reprimanded and/or prosecuted for bad behavior. The attention given to these celebrities sends a message to teens that it's cool to behave badly. Young males who are following these behavior patterns are, usually, struggling with their own identities, and they need to build up their fragile egos by calling attention to themselves in a dramatic way. In many cases, they are frustrated and don't have any goals or career interests. Some of them come from home environments that are troubled and broken with little or no parental oversight. Others, whether they know it or not, are modeling this behavior as a way of sending a covert cry for help in dealing with their inadequacies.

The rise of the 'gangsta culture' has been another iconic influence on the attitudes of young urban males. The glamorization of guns, fast money, and flamboyant lifestyles has lured many impressionable teens into thinking they can aspire to these false, shallow images. A number of young males have completely lost interest in school and their education as a result of these enticements.

The 'bad boy/bad girl' images that have been portrayed in the media have given credence to some of the negative social behavior that is demonstrated by many teens today. For example:

• The disrespect for all types of authority

• The lyrical denigration of women and lewd behavior

• The rise in male aggression towards each other

• The increased use of handguns and criminal activity

Peers and associates who subscribe to these actions and behavior oftentimes possess low self-esteem and low expectations about life. They mask their insecurities by doing whatever it takes to 'fit-in', i.e., drugs, crime, risky sexual behavior, and so on. They engage in these activities without regard for the long-term consequences of their behavior. These individuals enjoy using peer pressure tactics to get other people to participate in malicious or risky behavior with them. The more people they enlist, the more they can justify their actions and behavior, and this provides them with a false sense of acceptance and power. Feeding into their pressure is dangerous and jeopardizes the credibility and the self-respect of anyone who succumbs to their wishes.

If you find yourself in the company of peers who feel this way or who are moving in this direction, then you need to make some changes. This may be a difficult break to make, especially if you're in a vulnerable place in your life, you don't make new friends easily, or if you like your peers, but just don't like their behavior. Keep in mind, while you may like your friends, if their behavior is malicious or self-destructive, it could lead to consequences that you may not be willing or able to handle. Standing up to negative friends and peers can be challenging, but hold fast to your values and principles should you encounter any conflicts. Where possible, get the support of friends or peers, who share your beliefs, to stand with you. If you feel guilty or have problems breaking away from negative peers, find a reliable role-model, guidance counselor, or mentor to help you make the transition. Don't forget about your parents and other family members; they can also be a great resource for support. It is also very critical that you learn to trust yourself and rely on your own choices and decisions. In any event, never let anyone pressure you into compromising your principles or your judgment to gain their approval or acceptance. Anyone who tries to do so does not have your best interest at heart. Believing in yourself and having faith in your abilities is the impetus you need to accomplish your goals and resist the effects of negative peer pressure.

Exercise 4

1. What are some of the dangers of negative peer pressure?

_____

_____

_____

2. Describe some of your experiences with negative peer pressure

_____

_____

_____

3. What were some of the effects? How did you react to it?

_____

_____

_____

4. In what ways does negative peer pressure compromise your choices, your decisions?

_____

_____

_____

5. Have you ever participated in a situation where someone was physically abused by the actions of you and/or your peers? If so, how did you feel before, during and afterwards?

_____

_____

_____

6. What were the consequences, if any?

_____

_____

_____

7. List some instances where you resisted negative peer pressure. What tactics did you use to stand up against it? How did it make you feel in each situation?

_____

_____

_____

Gangs and Peer Pressure

As stated earlier, your peers can be your allies or your foes…Gangs are your foes!

They are one of America's biggest problems. Since their evolution, they have destroyed lives and ruined neighborhoods. Not a day goes by that we don't see media coverage of the wretched effects of their influence. Drugs, guns, and the daily killing of young men have all taken their toll on communities around the country. You probably know someone who is involved or affiliated with a gang. Their power and influence crosses all ethnic lines, and they prey on young males who are insecure, from fragmented, economically deprived homes, and are looking for acceptance and belonging.

They're not a new phenomenon, but what has changed is their devices. The primary focus these days is making money by illicit means, such as gun trafficking, stealing, selling drugs, prostitution, and so on. They lure many young males under the guise of being a second family that will care for and protect them. They recruit vulnerable males through the enticement of drugs, fast money, and guns. Their influence rivals no other force. They use peer pressure frequently to get new recruits, and, if necessary, they will resort to physical harassment.

If you are depressed, unsure of yourself, don't have clear direction about your life, or you feel misunderstood, then it is of utmost importance that you avoid any offers to join a gang. The stakes are high, and your life will never be the same if you do. Once you're in, it's almost impossible to get out and they rule with an iron hand. Are you considering the possibility of becoming a gang member? Understand, as part of the initiation process, you may be asked to do things that compromise every principle that you've been taught. For example, you may get 'stomped', (severely beaten from heavy boots worn by gang members), as part of your initiation, told to destroy private property, or be required to kill an innocent person to prove your loyalties. The consequences of these loyalties could lead to long-term imprisonment or worse, death! If you have been approached to join a gang but have no interest in doing so, then be very careful how you decline the offer. They don't take rejection very well! If you are physically harassed or your life is threatened, here are some suggestions to help you handle the situation:

- First of all, remain calm. Don't feed into any arguments or aggressive behavior.

- If its during school hours, then contact someone in authority right away, teachers, guidance counselors, or the principle.

- If you're in a public place, still remain calm, politely back away from any confrontation, and try to get support from friends or peers in the vicinity to stand with you.

- Make parents and/or family members aware of the problem, and if warranted, notify the police of your situation and ask for their suggestions.

- Shy away from any activity that might suggest you are interested in becoming a gang member, e.g., wearing colors or clothes that emulate gang attire, using their symbolism, etc.

Whatever you do, don't try to resolve the problem on your own! Gangs are very dangerous, and, as you may know, they will seriously hurt or kill anyone who challenges them or gets in their way. Resisting the influence of peer pressure from gangs takes great courage and savvy. If improperly handled, you could jeopardize your life, or possibly, the life of someone close to you! Yes, if they can't get to you, they will go after people you care about - just to hurt you! They have no conscience when it comes to retaliation! The best thing to do is to avoid any encounters or associations with these individuals. Seek out peer groups that desire the best for you and your life. Pursue goals and objectives that will continually nurture and enhance your mental, emotional, spiritual and social well-being. Believe in yourself and maintain integrity in all that you do.

Exercise 5:

1. Discuss the dangers of gangs and their influence.

_____

_____

_____

2. How have gangs impacted your community? Your schools, neighborhoods, etc?

_____

_____

_____

3. Discuss gang-related crimes that happen on a regular basis in your neighborhood. How does it make you feel? What ideas would you suggest to resolve the problems?

_____

_____

_____

4. Discuss how gang membership affects your choices, your independence.

_____

_____

_____

5. List some names of friends and associates who were victims of gang-related incidents, e.g. shootings, beatings, killings.

_____

_____

_____

6. Were any of these friends or peers gang members? Wanna-be gang members, or innocent victims?

_____

_____

_____

7. Have you or your peers ever considered joining a gang? Why? Why not?

_____

_____

_____

8. List some of the factors to consider when resisting peer pressure from gangs.

_____

_____

_____

Reading Resources:

Coping With Peer Pressure, http://www.guidanceassociates.com

Peer Influence and Peer Relationships, http://www.focusas.com/PeerInfluence.html

Teens and Gangs, http://www.hopefs.org/Behavior/TeensandGangs.html

Peer Pressure, http://www.healthline.com/peer-pressure

ABOUT THE AUTHOR

GAIL L. FREDRICK

Gail L. Fredrick, a resident and native of Orlando, Florida, has over 25 years experience working within the construction industry. She is a Florida Certified Roofing Contractor, and President of Weeks Roofing Company. As a woman, working in a non-tradition field, she has been forced to face many unique challenges, which only enhanced her desire to achieve.

Ms. Fredrick also serves as Director of Finance and Administration for KTD Consulting Engineers, which specializes in mechanical, electrical, plumbing, and fire protection design services. She oversees all financial responsibilities, human resource functions, and supervises all administrative personnel.

Ms. Fredrick holds a Bachelor of Science degree in Business Management and Marketing. She is a former president, of the Greater Orlando Chapter of the National Association of Women In Construction, an association that promotes and enhances the success of women in the construction industry. She has earned the Construction Industry Technician certification, which acknowledges the accomplishment of attaining a high professional level in the construction industry.

Through her affiliation with the Professional Women's Network (PWN), she has been certified as a Business Coach, and enjoys sharing her knowledge and experience with those hoping to become entrepreneurs.

I dedicate this chapter to the young man in my life, my son, Brian. May you find your passion and achieve great success.

Contact:
Gail L. Fredrick, CIT
5269 Rocking Horse Place
Oviedo, Florida 32765
407.701.8629
gfredrick@cfl.rr.com

NINE

CHECKLIST FOR STARTING YOUR OWN BUSINESS

By Gail L. Fredrick

An entrepreneur can be defined as a person who seeks to capitalize on new and profitable endeavors or business, usually with considerable initiative and risk.

Starting a business is a huge undertaking, which requires an understanding of what it takes to start and keep a business running from its successful launch to its everyday operation. Many business ventures fail within the first few years because there is not sufficient research and planning conducted, prior to the start up. Success does not happen automatically, it requires hard work and dedication. For those individuals that possess the characteristics and commitment, the rewards can be beneficial, perhaps creating a life-changing situation.

This chapter will highlight a checklist of ten areas that are essential in the launch and operation of your business. There is plenty of research available to further assist you, and I encourage you to pursue this information on your own. Evaluate your personal characteristics and motivations, and then research business plan development, legal structures, licensing and business taxation, insurance, employment laws, and technology extensively. If you are considering the possibility of becoming a business owner or entrepreneur, you must be equipped with the knowledge to properly start and maintain a successful business. The following checklist will be a valuable resource to ensure the success of your business.

CHECKLIST FOR STARTING & **OPERATING YOUR OWN BUSINESS**
☑ Personal Evaluation
☑ Research and Planning
☑ Formulation of Business Plan
☑ Legal Structure
☑ Licensing and Business Taxes
☑ Insurance and Business Protection
☑ Staffing and Employment Laws
☑ Technology and Record Keeping
☑ Professionalism and Expectations
☑ Evaluation and Continuing Education

Personal Evaluation

Do you have what it takes? Do you possess the characteristics required to operate and manage your own business? Successful entrepreneurs typically have a number of similar skills and characteristics. It is critical for anyone considering starting a business to conduct a realistic and honest evaluation to determine skills, experience, values, personality, and motivation. Additionally, success will depend on your ability and willingness to sacrifice, and your degree of optimism and dedication. Regardless of your prior experience and knowledge, there are still risks associated with starting a new business. All risks cannot be identified in the beginning, and require initiative and problem-solving skills to overcome. You must be willing to take risks if you are to become a successful entrepreneur.

1. What do you consider to be your greatest strengths and weaknesses?

   _____

2. Are you willing to spend your time and financial resources to develop the business?

   _____

3. Are you able to develop relationships and work with others easily?

   _____

4. Are you motivated, a self-starter, and able to follow through on commitments?

   _____

5. Do you seek opportunities and not afraid to take risks?

_____

You must be able to visualize the results of your efforts. People choose business ownership for a variety of reasons, including independence, financial security, flexibility, and personal satisfaction. Having a passion for your business is crucial. You will be spending many hours working to ensure that the business is successful. The path that leads to success must be an enjoyable experience or your drive will be lost quickly. Clearly defining your goals will help you to stay committed, focused, and motivated as you work towards your objectives and achieve success. The following questions can be used as a basis to evaluate the feasibility of your business venture, as well as starting you on the path to defining your goals and aspirations.

1. What do I wish to gain from this business venture?

_____

2. How much time and effort am I willing to sacrifice to ensure its success?

_____

3. Can this business venture become the answer to fulfillment of my goals and aspirations?

_____

4. Will I enjoy working this business on a daily basis?

_____

Research and Planning

Is your product or service in demand? You must determine if there is a need or market for your particular product or service. If there are no customers or clients to buy your products or services, the business will not survive very long. You will spend endless hours promoting, and the result will be frustration. Entrepreneurs who perform their research and develop realistic plans are successful. Knowledge is essential. You should learn everything you can about your business; become an expert.

Clearly define your target market, and know your competition. Learning what makes each competitor unique will be important in the development of your promotional plans. Today, customers are more educated than ever before. By performing a few clicks, the Internet has changed target markets, from local to global. Customers have easy access to information, which has resulted in businesses having to become more creative to remain competitive. The uniqueness of your business will ultimately be the key to its success. What will you do to ensure your business stands out among your competitors? What is unique about your product or service?

Identify potential challenges and develop a plan to overcome these temporary obstacles. Owners sometimes think they are too busy to take the time to plan effectively, and find themselves just "going with the flow". This type of thinking is not healthy for the business, and could lead to failure. Your chances of success increases in direct relation to the time spent on planning and preparation. Lack of planning and the failure to perform sufficient market research are two of the biggest mistakes made by start-up businesses. Examine all the "what if" questions that come to mind, and plan accordingly.

1. What if I get sick and unable to make that deadline?

_____

2. What if my supplier is unable to deliver a needed part or product?

_____

3. What if the computer network crashes at a critical time?

_____

Formulation of a Business Plan (including Marketing and Financials)

The purpose of a business plan is to create the road map, which you will follow to ensure the success of your business. This is the initial instrument that begins the vital planning aspect. Completing the business plan will force you to evaluate and answer questions about what you hope to accomplish and how you will do so. The plan will be the standard utilized to identify your direction and accomplishments as you move forward. If you hope to obtain funding to start your business, a clearly defined business plan will be required by your lender.

There are many software packages and websites available to assist you in writing a business plan. However, no one can write the business plan for you. It must be a well thought out and well written plan that documents your aspirations and the methods used to achieve them. I encourage you to review prepared business plans of other companies prior to completion of your own. This will give you an idea of suggested content and detail needed to write an effective plan. There may be seminars or workshops available in your area that will assist you. Although this is a time-consuming task, it is vital to ensure your business achieves and maintains its success.

A typical business plan includes:

- Executive Summary – 1-2 page that summarizes the key points of the plan

- Description of Business – location, history, ownership and legal structure, key source of supplies

- Management and Organizational – personnel structure, skills and experience, outside advisors, subcontractors or suppliers

- <u>Market Plan</u>

- Industry – size of industry and revenue

- Product or Service – describe product or service

- Market Analysis – customers and competitors, how you compare

- Market Strategy – how you will target, promote and attract customers

- <u>Financial Plan</u>

- Historical Financial Statements – income statement, balance sheet, cash flow analysis

- Monthly Projections – revenue, expenses, and cash flow needs, break-even

- Funding – amount needed and how funds will be used, source of funds

- <u>Appendix</u>

- Resumes – owners and/or management team

- Legal Documents – business license, professional licenses, articles of incorporation

Legal Structure

There are many factors to consider in the formulation of a new business. If the new business set-up is not handled properly initially, serious ramifications could occur that adversely affect the business and/or the business owner, both financially and legally. As a business owner, it will be necessary to wear many hats. It is not advisable or necessary to attempt to operate the business alone. Seek the advice of professionals. At the minimum, I strongly encourage you to seek the professional advice of a lawyer and accountant. There are many forms of business ownership and you must determine if your business will be a sole proprietorship, a partnership, a C-corporation, an S-corporation, or a limited liability company. Additionally, a banker, realtor, insurance agent, and marketing consultant may be necessary.

Licensing and Business Taxes

Based on the type of legal structure you have selected for your business, there will be certain federal requirements. A federal identification number may be assigned by completing IRS Form SS-4. Businesses must file an annual tax return, based on the business' fiscal period, which was recorded at the time of application for the federal identification number. Assistance from your accountant will be necessary to complete the returns correctly. The annual return will also be dependent on the type of legal structure you have chosen. All businesses are required to pay and submit unemployment taxes at both the state and federal level, as well as social security and Medicare tax. Sole proprietors, partnerships, and some limited liabilities will also be responsible for self-employment tax.

Depending on the type of business and the state in which it will be located, requirements for state licensing and taxes will vary accordingly. Most states require the registration of a fictitious name for the business. A fictitious business name allows you to legally operate as a DBA (do business as), a name associated with the business, other than your full legal name. Other possible licensing and tax reporting may include corporate tax, state income tax, and sales taxes. It is imperative that extensive research be conducted to obtain the specific requirements for your location. Seek assistance from your accountant.

Typically, at the local level (city or county), businesses are required to obtain a business or occupational license, which officially registers the business name and location within the city or county. A visit to the local zoning office may be needed to ensure the business accommodates the appropriate zoning requirements for the area. Copies of other licenses, which document education and/or experience, may also be required.

Certain professionals are required to satisfy educational prerequisites before a business can be started. These may be in the form of degrees earned at accredited universities or a state administered exam in many industries, such as realtors, doctors, or contractors. Completion of professional education units or continuing education credits are needed for license renewals and to ensure the licensee continues to stay current on industry standards.

Insurance and Business Protection

Unknowns and uncertainties are known as risks. Risks involve taking a chance that could result in a gain or loss. The loss could be in the form of time, money, life, or some other resource. Your business will be providing a product or service to the general public, and it is expected that no harm will become of the exchange. However, things do happen that no one can expect. Insurance is a necessary expense to the business that protects both the business and the public. In many cases, proof of insurance will be required before business can be conducted.

A business may purchase a combination of insurance coverage from the many types of insurance. Liability insurance protects the business against claims resulting from the operations of the business, either bodily injury or property damage to a third party. Workers compensation protects employees against injury while working on the job. Professional liability insurance, purchased by licensed professionals, is a requirement to conduct business and protects against claims arising as a result of provided services. Other types of business insurance include medical, property, flood/windstorm, officer liability, renters, automobile, errors and omissions, and key man.

If your business has developed an intellectual concept or process, or some type of invention, this needs to be protected from duplication. Patents, copyrights trademark or service mark registrations provide protection to the business or inventor. A patent protects an original device or process. Copyrights protect items such as printed material, consulting manuals, books, and computer software. Trademarks and service marks guard a product or service name, logo, symbol, or figure.

Staffing and Employment Laws

Before you hire a staff to support your business, thorough knowledge of both labor and tax laws should be gained. Ignorance could result in excessive fines or legal ramifications with employees and/or the federal government. Employee payroll, although deductible as a business expense, adds additional operating costs to the business. Careful analysis should be conducted to determine the feasibility and necessity of hiring a staff. Some businesses will require a full staff to operate, such as manufacturing. In some cases, independent contractors or consultants could be hired on a limited basis to assist with special projects, hence, eliminating the payroll tax liability.

Employers are required by federal law to pay one-half of an employee's Social Security and Medicare tax. Additionally, federal income tax must be deducted and deposited with the Internal Revenue Service. State income tax deductions may also be required, for many states. Also, mentioned previously, state and federal unemployment tax is paid by employers, based on earned wages. A state issued employer identification number will be required for unemployment tax reporting.

Seek employees that will promote the business professionally and possess the characteristics that will enhance the businesses' image and reputation. Hire an employee with a good attitude, who is ambitious, and is motivated to work as a team member. Be sure there is a clearly defined job description for each employee, for which they can be accountable. Treat your employees well, as their contentment will reflect on your customers and clients.

Technology and Record Keeping

Computers and other technology will be needed to ensure speed, accuracy, documentation and professionalism. Will you be writing contracts, designing brochures, or tracking inventory? Technology and record keeping are linked directly. An accounting software package will organize and maintain financial records. Financial information will be used to evaluate the current condition of the business and forecast for the future.

Evaluate your needs for computer hardware and software, and research thoroughly before making these purchases. Costs associated with these purchases could be excessive, but are necessary to ensure sufficient record keeping, as well as tools to properly operate your business. Accurate record keeping will save you lots of time, money, and embarrassment. Other necessary equipment may include a copier or printer, scanner, fax machine, and telephones.

Once you begin your business, it is critical that you maintain records that are both complete and organized. There will be times when copies of company documents will be required for banks and others you wish to do business with. Examples of documentation you will need to keep and have readily available include:

- Legal Documents (business licenses, fictitious business name statement, partnership agreement, articles of incorporation or organization, resellers permit, documents recorded with your state)

- Banking Information (monthly statements and cancelled checks, etc)

- Unpaid Invoices (accounts receivables)

- Paid Invoices (collected revenue)

- Unpaid Bills (accounts payable)

- Paid Bill Receipts

- Receipts for Purchased Items

- Contracts for Projects or Clients

- Employee Personnel Files

- Payroll Records

- Tax Records

Professionalism and Expectations

One of the keys to building a successful business is developing a network of happy and satisfied customers. Satisfied customers will want to conduct business with you again, and refer you to others. You are challenged as a new business owner to develop a relationship with your customer, one that builds trust and exemplifies your professionalism and integrity. Attempt to do everything within your power to ensure this relationship remains intact. Do what you say you will do, when you say you will do it. Be prepared for meetings, be on time, and return calls promptly. Eliminate any reason for people to think less of you.

Customer service is the "life blood" of your business. If your business cannot provide support and customer service, your customer will seek one of your competitors that will provide this benefit. Make sure that everyone in your organization is properly trained in customer service skills, and realizes the importance of developing and maintaining strong customer relationships.

Everyone has heard the saying, "Don't judge a book by its cover." Unfortunately, this is not true in the business world. Your appearance is part of your marketing package. First impressions do count, and your appearance makes a statement about the quality of work one can expect to receive from you. You may want to consider hiring a professional marketing consultant to coach you in this area.

Evaluation and Continuing Education

You must develop performance measurements that monitor your business, its health, and its progress. If you do not track and monitor your business, how will you determine its condition and success? Performance measurements are one of the keys to long-term growth. These results will guide in changing, revising, or implementing new processes or procedures, which enhance the operation of the business. Having the proper technology and software in place will simplify and expedite this process.

Compare your current business to your written business plan. Are you following the path you identified earlier? Are you realizing those goals you had anticipated? Are sales increasing in quality of customer and quantity? Are customers satisfied? Is there sufficient cash available for expenses? Are you making a profit? These are examples of questions, as well as others, you will want to evaluate often.

Of great importance to your business is the commitment of its owner and management team to the concept of continuing education. You must stay educated on new laws, technology, products, ideas, or services that affect your business and its operation. New information that pertains to the industry that your business is involved is also critical. Read printed publications, subscribe to industry newsletters, or search the Internet to increase your knowledge.

Become active in local associations that provide speakers and seminars relating to your area of interest. These associations are also beneficial in developing communication, leadership skills, time management, etc, also vital skills needed to manage and operate a business. Strive to stay a foot ahead of your competition, in both skill and knowledge. The success of your business is dependent upon it.

Reading Resources:

Business Plans www.bplans.com

Domain Names www.register.com or www.networksolutions.com

Emarketer www.emarketer.com

Entrepreneur Reference www.entrepreneur.com

EntreWorld www.entreworld.com

Inc. Magazine www.inc.com

Internal Revenue Services www.irs.gov

SCORE www.score.org

U. S. Bureau of Census www.census.gov

U. S. Copyright Office www.copyright.gov

U. S. Department of Commerce www.doc.gov

U. S. Department of Labor www.dol.gov

U. S. Department of Labor, Occupational Safety & Health Administration www.osha.gov

U. S. Department of Justice: Americans with Disabilities Act www.ada.gov

U. S. Equal Employment Opportunity Commission www.eeoc.gov

U. S. Federal Government www.business.gov

U. S. Patent and Trademark Office www.uspto.gov

U.S. Small Business Administration www.sba.gov

Wall Street Journal www.wsj.com

Working Solo www.workingsolo.com

Young Entrepreneurs www.teenvestor.com

Notes:

ABOUT THE AUTHOR

AHMON`DRA (BRENDA) McCLENDON

Ahmon`dra, President of Brilliance Inc., is an international speaker, facilitator, motivator and author. She imprints an indelible impression upon your heart and makes you smile, laugh, cry and contemplate the deeper issues of life. She arouses in each listener a passion to commit to his or her higher purpose with her grace, power and spirit.

With twenty plus years in the human services arena and an MSW from San Francisco State University, Ahmon`dra has developed a highly successful program called P.L.A.N.E. – "Passionately Living A New Existence." She has spoken to thousands of young adults in North America, Europe and Africa on how to create a powerful future by staying devoted to their dreams, trusting their intuition, boldly taking risks and asking for what they want.

She is a Certified Facilitator for Motivating the Teen Spirit Inc. a teen empowerment program that conducts transformational workshops, and leads the international program, Core Value Training as a Senior Instructor. Ahmon`dra is a recipient of the "Speaking with an Active Voice" grant sponsored by the American Medical Women's Association and Pharmacia Corporation.

A contributing author to the best selling book *Chicken Soup For the African-American Soul*, she was featured as a keynote speaker for The Monster Diversity 2003 Leadership Program in the United States.

Passion and magnificence exude from her presence with an amazing energy of wisdom, healing & love as she creates, flies and soars! Get clear on your life and passions with the energy and excitement of Ahmon`dra

Contact
Ahmon`dra (Brenda) McClendon
Brilliance, Inc.
484 Lakepark Ave pmb 485
Oakland, California 94610
Ahmondra@aol.com
www.protrain.net

TEN

WHAT'S YOUR DREAM? CHARTING YOUR PLAN OF ACTION

By Ahmon'dra McClendon

Destiny Awaits, Young Men!

Be bold, take action and create a life _you_ love! It doesn't matter who you are or where you come from, the power to achieve your dreams is in your hands.

The legendary rapper, poet, writer and actor Tupac Shakur stated, _"Reality is wrong. Dreams are for real."_ He understood that life is not determined by what you see or what you hear; it is determined by what you think and feel. The moment you realize you are not your circumstances and that your past does not dictate your future, the door to possibilities swings open.

Steve Walker, a twenty-two-year old successful business executive, summed it up nicely when he wrote, _"Be pro-active. Don't wait for things_ *to fall into your lap, because waiting begets waiting. I waited for something to happen to me for almost three years, until I decided to **MAKE** something happen for myself."*

Play to Win!

The Game of Life is not a spectator sport, and only those who actively play can win. There are two kinds of participants in life: spectators and players.

Spectators observe life passively from the sidelines and never get directly involved. They criticize the accomplishments of others because they have little going for themselves. Spectators complain about the unfairness of life, and hide their fears and disappointments behind hateful attitudes.

Players, on the other hand, are actively involved in life. They identify what's important, move past their fears, and accept their circumstances and live life on purpose. Players maintain positive attitudes, and never allow failed attempts to kill their dreams. No matter what challenges arise, players stay focused. They always take the initiative and make personal sacrifices when needed. To them, life is a game worth winning.

NBA star Allen Iverson is a great example of a serious "player". When he found himself off the courts and in a prison cell at the age of eighteen, he refused to sit and watch life pass him by. Even though he lost a scholarship from Kentucky State, he chose to remain in the game. He accepted the situation, gathered strength from the experience, and continued to move forward toward his dream.

What relationship do you have with life?

Do you sit on the sidelines and watch like a spectator?

Are you actively engaged in making life happen like a player?

Is it time to step up your game and become a more effective player?

In this chapter, it is my intention to help you develop a "winning strategy for life". And no matter what level you are currently playing, you will have the opportunity to:

1. Identify your dreams and list what is truly important.

2. Clarify your belief systems and list possible roadblocks to success.

3. Create an action plan and list the steps necessary to realize your dreams.

Know What You Want!

A dream is a desire that, when achieved, brings fulfillment and happiness to your life. Before you can live your dreams, you have to *identify* your dreams. Living a life you love means experiencing happiness in all areas of your life.

Activity #1—Identify Your Dreams.

Identify a specific dream for each area of your life. It is possible to realize a dream in one area, yet be unfulfilled in another. You may gain financial freedom and be unhappy with your relationships.

Ex. I dream of having (family) a close relationship with my sister.

Ex. I dream of having (financial) a best selling book that generates two million dollars in sales.

I dream of having (financial)

_____

I dream of having (career)

_____

I dream of having (family)

_____

I dream of having (health)

_____

I dream of having (social)

_____

I dream of having (emotional)

_____

I dream of having (society)

_____

I dream of having (_____)

_____

I dream of having (_____)

_____

I dream of having (_____)

_____

I dream of having (_____)

_____

Know Who You Are!

The only force that can hold you back or move you forward in life is *you*. Once you know where you want to go, identify those attitudes or beliefs that could hold you back or sidetrack your progress.

Activity #2—Clarify Your Belief System.
The opportunity of a lifetime can slip by because you allow personal fears or prejudices to get in the way. List all the personal beliefs or opinions that could negatively influence your decisions. Take each negative belief and develop it into a positive opinion. Repeat the positive opinions regularly until you form a new positive belief system.

Ex. I believe that I don't have a chance because I am poor.
Ex. I believe that I have a chance because I am getting an education.

I believe that_____

I believe that_____

I have _____

I have _____

I am _____

I am _____

Take any statement that is true for you and create a positive statement to replace it.

I believe I was born unlucky because_____.

I believe that my opportunities are limited.

I believe my _____ is holding me back.

(race, gender, criminal record, family, etc.)

I have fears about my_____.

(past, current situation, future, living situation, etc.)

I believe that my dreams are out of my reach.

I have trouble asking for and accepting support.

I am easily influenced by the negative opinions of others.

I have a _____ problem I need to handle it.

(fill in the blank: drug, anger, fear, etc.)

I believe my life is bad and getting worse.

I believe my life is hopeless.

(Create your own statements)

_____

_____

_____

Know Where You're Going!

When you do not have a game plan for life, you don't have direction. Not being clear about your direction can allow others to impose their agenda upon you. You could find yourself participating in activities that do not serve you. Not having a strategy in life can be destructive.

Activity #3—Create an Action Plan.

1. Make a list of all your dreams.
2. For each dream, list the tasks required to fulfill it.
3. List the resources you will need.
4. List all possible roadblocks.
5. List all the positive rewards you will gain from realizing your dream.

Ex. DREAM: I have a dream of writing a best selling book.

To realize this dream, I will need: *To write the book and have it edited.*

To realize this dream, I will need: *To identify a publisher.*

I believe a roadblock to my success could be: My *procrastination and negative thinking.*

I believe a positive reward could be: *Financially making good money.*

Not reaching my dream will: *Cause me to feel like a failure, and keep me from sharing my knowledge with others.*

My reward for reaching my Dream is: *My self-esteem will rise, I will make money, and I will make a positive impact on the world*

(Complete the exercise for each dream, and be specific.)

DREAM: _____

To realize this dream I will need:_____

To realize this dream I will need:_____

I believe a roadblock to my success could be: _____

I believe a roadblock to my success could be: _____

Not reaching my dream will: _____

Not reaching my dream will: _____

My reward for reaching my Dream is: _____

My reward for reaching my Dream is: _____

DREAMS DO MAKE A DIFFERANCE!

A dream can begin as a personal desire, evolve into a world-changing event, and impact the lives of thousands. That was the case with 16-year-old Ryan White, who turned a personal dream into a world wide educational campaign on AIDS. In a testimony to the President's commission on AIDS, Ryan shared his story.

"I came face to face with death at thirteen years old. I was diagnosed with AIDS: a killer. Given six months to live and being the fighter that I am, I set high goals for myself. It was my decision to live a normal life, go to school, be with my friends, and enjoy day-to-day activities. It was not going to be easy."

And it wasn't easy for Ryan. He was ostracized at school. His locker was vandalized, he had to use a separate restroom, a separate drinking fountain, disposable eating utensils, and he wasn't allowed to attend gym classes. Eventually, his family had to move from his hometown because of the discrimination, but Ryan never gave up. When he died in 1990, he had turned an incurable disease and a personal dream into a way to educate the world about AIDS. He single-handedly changed school system policies, and made it possible for other students with AIDS to live with respect and dignity. Despite the odds against him, Ryan remained a "player" to the end.

What is Really Happening?

The following statements were made by young men who are "players" in the game of life. Have your close associates complete the questions, and use the answers to identify the spectators and players in your life.

If you could do anything in your life, what would it be?

Alfred, age 16: 1/27/91 —"*Rewrite all the wrongs in my life.*"
DeRon, age 16: 7/23/91 —"*Graduate from a four-year university and have a functional family.*"

Branden, age 17: 6/20/90 —"*I would help others and be a mentor.*"
Dynell, age 16: 2/16/91 —"*I would go back with my family.*"

Name one thing that could keep you from reaching your goals?

Justin, age 17: 8/22/90 —"*Getting put in jail for making quick money.*"
Aaron, age 18: 10/7/89 —"*Dropping out of school.*"

Steve. age 22: 3/8/85 —*"Having self-doubt."*

Name one thing that you could do to reach your goals?
Gerald, age 17: 10/3/90 — *"Stay in school."*
Steve, age 22: 3/8/85 — *"Not giving up when things get hardest. Not taking the easy way out."*
Branden, age 17: 6/20/90 — *"Keeping myself strong mentally."*

What advice do you have for young men trying to make it?
Branden, age 17: 6/20/90 — *"Find a source of support."*
Steve, age 22: 3/8/85 — *"Don't give the world the opportunity to change who you are. This is your opportunity to change the world."*
Aaron, age 18: 10/07/89 — *"Stay out of trouble and stay involved in positive activities."*
Mikai, age 10: 8/6/97 — *"Stay in school and don't let your actions ruin your life."*
Robert, age 16: 10/15/91 — *"Stay out of gangs and keep your head up."*
Gerald, age 17: 10/3/90 — *"Stay focused."*
Alfred, age 16: 1/27/91 — *"Do what you can do and do it with your heart."*

Stay On Purpose and Realize Your Dreams.

Everyone has a purpose in life, and living that purpose will bring you happiness. Keep moving forward and staying active. Don't live life from the sidelines as a spectator. Be vigilant, stay alert, and when challenges arise, meet them with a "Player" attitude.

"If you want to be treated like a grown man, you need to act like a grown man. Don't act like an idiot, just because you want to be accepted and considered "cool". There are far worse things in life than not being "cool", and wasting you life is one of them."
—Steve Walker

"I know it seems hard sometimes but remember one thing. Through every dark night, there's a bright day after that. So no matter how hard it get(s), stick your chest out, keep ya head up.... and handle it."

"During your life, never stop dreaming. No one can take away your dreams."
—Tupac Shakur

Notes:

_____

_____

_____

_____

_____

_____

_____

_____

_____

_____

_____

_____

_____

_____

_____

_____

_____

_____

_____

_____

ABOUT THE AUTHOR

HANNAH CRUTCHER

Hannah Crutcher, President and CEO of Hannah Crutcher & Associates, is an educator with over twenty years of experience in higher education. Most of that experience is in career counseling and job placement at six colleges and universities. Her passion for eduction extends to K-12 students as well; she has served as a Brownie Girl Scout troop leader, and president, treasurer, and secretary in the Parent/Teachers Association. Hannah is also a member of the Professional Women's Network International Advisory Board.

Ms. Crutcher received a Bachelor's degree in Speech Education with a minor in drama; she loves live theater and has appeared in such classics as *The Amen Corner*, *The Women*, and *The Merry Widow*. She has a Master's degree in Management and is a certified seminar trainer with particular interest in leadership skills, sales, and customer service.

She and her husband Melvin have been married for thirty years and have two adult children.

Contact:
Hannah Crutcher & Associates
1605 Germantown Parkway
Suite 111-216
Cordova, Tennessee 38016
(901) 604-1700
(901) 753-3988 (Fax)
crutcherf@bellsouth.net
www.protrain.net

ELEVEN

BEING RESPONSIBLE: DATING, JOBS, PARENTS

By Hannah Crutcher

Growing up is sometimes tough for everyone; as a young man, you have your own unique set of challenges to overcome. The good thing about growing up is that it is a time for learning from your mistakes, and taking corrective action to change behavior or habits. The tough part about growing up is that the mistakes can be quite painful and costly; so, it is very essential to have a plan and stay focused on what is important to you. One of the best ways to do this is to find a mentor and work diligently with this person to set and always work toward some personal goals.

Exercise:

Ask yourself the following questions:

1. What is a mentor?

    Write your definition.

    _____

    _____

    _____

    Find the definition of "mentor" in a dictionary and write it down.

    _____

    _____

    _____

2. List the names of people who you think would be a good mentor to you.

    _____

    _____

    _____

3. List qualities these people have that make them a good mentor.

    _____

    _____

    _____

Being Responsible and Accountable for Your Actions

Everyone makes mistakes growing up and in adulthood; this is just human nature. Making mistakes is inevitable; how and when you correct your mistakes could drastically change the direction of your life's journey. Being accountable and owning up to your actions is one of the most important things you can do – **always**!

Your action or reaction to a mistake is a direct reflection of your character. By the time you reflect on a mistake, you have had a chance to consider exactly what happened, what steps need to be taken now, and then proceed to do whatever you can to change the situation.

Why Should You Be Concerned About Being Accountable for Your Actions?

Accountability:

- Helps you define who you are

- Helps you set standards for yourself and others

- Helps you be a better judge of character

Exercise:

1. Think about a time when you believe you were not being accountable for your actions.

Describe the event in detail. Explain what happened to let you know you were not being accountable.

_____

_____

_____

2. Did you take any actions to correct what happened?

_____

_____

_____

3. If not, what actions do you wish you had taken?

_____

_____

_____

4. How do you think those actions would have helped?

_____

_____

_____

Why Being Responsible and Accountable Can Also Mean Being Unpopular

One of the biggest concerns facing a lot of teenagers and young adults is thinking they are not popular or do not "fit in." Sometimes being unpopular means you had to make an unpopular decision – the right decision. Making the right decision can sometimes be very painful, especially in the short-term, but the long-term effect can reap benefits for years to come.

Perhaps you possibly know someone who you consider very popular, seems to know all the right people, gets invited to all the right parties, and always says the right things. This person, however, may not be as happy as he looks or acts. Perhaps he spends so much time trying to fit in and make others like him that he doesn't even know who he is. Being liked and knowing that others like spending time with you is very important to everyone, but it should not come at any cost.

It is important to note, however, that there are many people who are sincerely popular and well liked by many because of their very nature. Usually, these are people who first liked themselves, and are able to get to know and truly like others. Their mere presence puts others at ease, and makes them feel comfortable and confident. Whenever you are fortunate enough to meet someone like this, study this person's habits and try to get to know him; this is the type of person you seek as a mentor. You do not have to necessarily spend a lot of time with him, but make sure the time you get does count. Mentors are the kind of people who are usually quite flattered that you have asked for their advice, and are quite willing to share their life's secrets with you.

Exercise:

1. **Think of a time you felt unpopular.** Now, list what exactly was going on in your life. What was your age at the time, who were your friends, and what kind of activities were you involved in with these friends?

_____

_____

_____

2. **What were some of the emotions you experienced feeling unpopular?**

_____

_____

_____

3. **Did you share these feelings with anyone?** If you shared these feelings, who was the person or people you shared them with? If not, why did you choose to keep these feelings bottled up inside?

_____

_____

_____

4. **What changes, if any, would you make the next time you need to deal with feeling unpopular?**

_____

_____

_____

Relationships

Dating

As you grow and mature, you'll find that you will develop more and more relationships. Most people become interested in dating and in developing close relationships. Dating can be a lot of fun and very exciting. It is a time when you can really get to know someone, and allow them to find out who you really are. It is a time of sharing your thoughts, feelings – and your time.

One of the most important things you can do for yourself and for the person you are dating is to have a real good idea of who you are: what you represent, your values, your hopes and dreams. Knowing who you are helps you make good decisions. It means that you have put in some time thinking about what's important to you and what actions you need to take in certain situations.

Also, it is important for you to know as much as you can about the person you are dating. While you do not want to appear pushy or nosy, just be very attentive and listen – you will be amazed at how much you can learn.

When both parties in a relationship are open and grounded:

• Sound decisions are more likely to be made.

• There is less conflict to deal with.

• There is more respect for each other.

• It can leads to better relationships with family and friends.

1. **How would you describe the ideal person for you to date?** Be very honest, and list all the features you want this person to have.

_____

_____

_____

2. **Are you currently in a relationship or dating someone?** If so, do you believe this is the right person for you? If not, please explain why.

_____

_____

_____

3. **What do you believe your role should be in this relationship?** Do you believe you are being honorable and respectful to this person? If not, why, and how do you plan to change things?

_____

_____

_____

4. **What do you believe is the toughest part about being in a relationship?**

_____

_____

_____

5. **Do you have a role model when it comes to dating?** If so, who is this person, and why did you choose him?

_____

_____

_____

Jobs

One of the most important things you will do, as you develop and mature, is to transition into the work world. These will truly be some of the most important relationships in your life. There are many teenagers and young adults who work and support themselves and others; most of these people will work for many years to come. Whether you are working part or full-time, whether your job is stacking boxes neatly on top of one another, or you are an expert in a certain field, treat your responsibilities with the utmost care and thoroughness.

Be even more conscientious how you treat the people you work for and with. Once again, it all comes back to accountability: knowing who you are and being true to yourself. When you know who you are and are happy with yourself, it is reflected in all your relationships.

Exercise:

1. **Are you currently employed? If not, have you been employed in the past?** If you answered yes to either question, what is/was your job title? Describe your duties. List what you like most about the job, and what you like least.

_____

_____

_____

2. **Do you find the work interesting? Is it something you want to do for a while?** If not, what steps do you think you need to take to get into the right line of work?

_____

_____

_____

3. **Have you set any goals that will help you in your present job, or help you find one you like more?** List your goals, and what steps you will take to reach them.

_____

_____

_____

4. **Take some time and think about your co-workers.** Think of someone you believe has a great work ethic and is a positive role model. List qualities this person has that make him/her a role model.

_____

_____

_____

5. **List any of the qualities of your role model that you possess as well.**

_____

_____

_____

Parents

Of all the relationships in your life, the ones you share with your parents will be the first and very likely the most significant ones in which you will be involved. The parental relationships set the tone for all the others; how you feel about yourself, and also how you feel about others, is in many cases the result of those relationships. Strong, nurturing parents help you secure your place in society; their love and support is immeasurable.

Like all other relationships, however, these relationships are only as strong as all the people involved. For that reason, you will probably have some conflict from time to time. This conflict is normal and probably unavoidable.

Exercise:

1. **Take some time and really think about one of the fondest memories you can remember with your father.** Now, describe it in detail; relive exactly what happened. How old were you, what did you do (go to the zoo, fishing)? Can you remember what you were wearing?

_____

_____

_____

2. **Think of one the fondest memories you can remember with your mother.** Perhaps it was a book you read together, or she helped you with a science project. List in detail exactly what happened during this special time.

_____

_____

_____

3. **Can you remember sharing a secret with your father or mother?** Explain what it meant to you – did you feel special or grown-up?

_____

_____

_____

4. **Do you remember a time when your father or mother said or did something that was very hurtful to you?** Perhaps they used some very harsh language to discipline you, and never said, "I'm sorry." Write exactly what was said, how you felt, and what you said. Describe if you felt helpless, insecure or unloved. Now describe how you wish things had happened, and how you will avoid this mistake as a parent.

_____

_____

_____

5. **Do you remember a time when you let your parents down?** Perhaps you were not completely open and honest about something. Can you remember the hurt you saw in their eyes? Describe the incident in detail. What was your age, what was going on in your life, why did you feel you could not go to your parents for advice before you got into trouble? Describe how you wish things had happened, resolve that there is conflict in all relationships, and you will show love and respect to your children, even when they are in trouble – **especially when they are in trouble!**

The importance of being accountable in your relationships with your parents cannot be overemphasized. Work hard everyday to know who you are, be responsible and accountable, and realize that the relationships you share with your parents will not only remain strong, but will grow and thrive, and be the foundation of relationships you will build and share with your children.

Being accountable and responsible for yourself and your choices is very important on your journey to manhood. May you find the inner strength and courage to always be honest with yourself and your values.

Recommended Reading:

Emotional Intelligence by Daniel Goleman

Rich Kid, Smart Kid by Robert T. Kiyosaki

Savage Inequalities – Children in America's Schools by Jonathan Kozol

ABOUT THE AUTHOR

April B. Jones

April Jones is President and CEO of A Plan For You, LLC. She conducts workshops and seminars that have been presented throughout the United States and abroad. The workshops and seminars conducted by the institute consist of topics such as: Women in Management, Women as Leaders, The Superwoman Syndrome, Leadership Skills, The Assertive Woman, Customer Service, Diversity and Emotional Wellness for Women. Ms. Jones has been certified by The Professional Woman Network as a Professional Coach and Diversity Consultant.

Ms. Jones' knowledge of business and professionalism is supported by working with corporations, non-profit and charity organizations. She has over 14 years of experience with the U.S. Federal Government in information technology and management, 7+ years consulting experience with churches and small business firms.

Among her many accomplishments, Ms. Jones has co-authored two books, been recognized by Strathmore's Who's Who Global Network for Outstanding Professionals, holds a Masters Degrees in Telecommunication and Information Systems from Capitol College in Laurel, Maryland and a Masters Degree in Information Management with a specialization in Government from Syracuse University in Syracuse, New York.

This chapter is dedicated to the most important and inspiring young man I know, my son, Graylin R. Walker, II.

Contact:
A Plan for You, LLC.
1282 Smallwood Drive W. #332
Waldorf, MD 20603
(301) 710.5421
Email: info@aplanforyou.org
www.aplanforyou.org
www.isthatyourhouse.com
www.protrain.net

TWELVE

PREPARING FOR COLLEGE AND A CAREER

By April Jones

Have you ever wanted to know what type of childhood successful men have had? What makes successful men tick? What type of sports they played as a child? Did they have 4.0 grade point averages? Did they know early in life what steps to take to become successful? How did they know to pursue that career path? What did they do to prepare? It is my hope that by the time you complete this chapter, I will have planted a seed that will continue to grow and eventually bloom throughout your life's travels. This is your template for college and career success.

"A Man of Knowledge Increases Power." —Proverbs 24:5

I have a son. When he was five, he wanted to be a fireman. Now that he's ten, he wants to be an NFL player. And somewhere in between,

153

he wanted to work at Bennigan's Restaurant and be paid with potato soup! I'm sure between now and his high school graduation, he'll have a few more career idea changes. What will be key for him and/or any other young man reading this chapter to understand is the importance of *planning* for college and/or career success, and that planning starts today!

The Foundation

The foundation for any type of preparation for the future is based upon your understanding of who you are, what is essential to you, and what your dreams and approach are for the future. This understanding can help you begin a process of decision-making about your future. Some simple questions can help you reflect on your life's success plan.

Ask yourself:

- What has triggered my moves in the past?

- What are the significant influences on my life, and how have they affected my career?

- What are my skills?

- What do I see as my strengths?

- What are my limitations?

- What have my successes and failures been?

- What are my core values?

- What are my current obligations and commitments?

- Do I have talents that I feel are underdeveloped?

- Do I feel as if I'm in a rut?

- Do my answers to these questions reflect an accurate picture? How do others see me?

College

The clock is ticking and the moment is here: that critical moment when your focus on college becomes more than just a thought. It's time to decide today!

A college degree is an expense that will more than pay for itself over your lifetime. As a young man with a college education, you will be afforded better job opportunities, paid more money, and expand skills and knowledge that can in no way be taken away. However, what you may not realize is that preparing for college shouldn't begin during your junior or senior year in high school. Your preparing for success as a college student should begin as soon as possible and continue through school age years. College preparation means planning for the future and making a number of significant decisions early on.

Employers want potential employees that have specific skill sets. But, did you know that the average university/college also expects enrolling students to have taken certain courses? The absolute best way for students to prepare for college is to take the appropriate courses and work to ensure they pass them. Your course schedule for each school year should be more challenging than the previous year. According to the U.S. Department of Education, college-bound students should take these courses:

- **Algebra I** and **Geometry,** or other demanding math classes that expect students to master the essentials of these subjects. These courses give students the skills they need to succeed on college entrance exams, in college math classes, and in their future careers.

- **English, Science and History, or Geography.** In addition to math, these classes make up your fundamental foundation. Every student should take English *each* year without exception. Science and history classes should be taken as much as possible.

- **Foreign Language.** Taking a foreign language demonstrates your level of commitment, and that you are serious and willing to learn more than simply the basics.

- **Computer Science.** Basic computer skills are now essential, and more and more jobs require at least a basic knowledge of computers. You should take advantage of any opportunities your school offers to learn computers.

- **The Arts.** Involvement in arts and music can be a valuable experience that widens your understanding and appreciation of the world.

How Much Will I Have To Pay?

The cost of a college or university degree will largely depend upon whether or not the school is public or private, and how long it takes you to complete the requirements for the degree. The average student will attend a state or public college. State and public schools obtain some of their funding from government agencies. Therefore, they charge lower rates for students who live in the same state (as the college or university). Students that live in states other that the home state for the university will pay higher rates. Private colleges and universities are likely to have higher rates than public colleges, regardless of in-state and out-of-state residency.

Determining the actual cost depends upon what year you plan to start college. By the time you leave for college, rates, room and board, and other miscellaneous fees may be higher than costs today. But keep in mind: as college and university rates go up, so does your potential salary upon completion of your degree, thus, your ability to repay any money you may need to borrow to attend school. There's no way to give you the exact amount you'll pay when it's time for you to go to college, but to get an idea of current rates for major colleges and universities in the United States, visit www.finaid.org/.

Financial aid is available from a number of sources for students, including the federal government, state governments, and the college and university they plan to attend. Aid can come from and be received from many avenues.

What Type Of Job Can I Get?

Examples of Jobs for Which a College Education May Be Required		
Two-Year College (Associate's Degree)	**Four-Year College** (Bachelor's Degree)	**Four Years or More** (Various Graduate Degrees Required)
Mechanical Engineer	Accountant	Architect
Cardiovascular Technician	Computer Systems Analyst	Biologist
Computer Technician	Dietitian	Chiropractor
Dental Hygienist	Editor	Dentist
Engineering Technician	Engineer	Doctor
Graphic Designer	FBI Agent	Economist
Heating, Air-Conditioning, and Refrigeration Technician	Investment Banker	Lawyer
Hotel or Restaurant Manager	Journalist	Paleontologist
Registered Nurse	Pharmacist	Psychologist
	Public Relations Specialist	Public Policy Analyst
	Therapist	Scientist
	Social Worker	University Professor
	Teacher	Veterinarian
		Zoologist

Career Planning

To have a successful career, you should do something you enjoy, something that will inspire you always. If once you graduate college (or high school) you have already decided your career path, don't be overwhelmed when making some of the hard decisions. Be sure to research your chosen occupation. Identify the stepping-stones and obstacles so you are prepared to make progress throughout the life cycle of your chosen occupation.

For example, if your chosen occupation is to become a physician, the life cycle for this field could look something like this:

Year One:	Intern
Years Two – Four:	Resident
Years Four+:	Chief Resident
Years Five+:	Attending

If you haven't quite decided your career path upon college (high school) graduation, don't panic. Realistically, career planning is often about making choices as you go. Very few successful people had any idea that they would end up where and how they did. These people learned from experiences encountered (both positive and negative) along the way, and made choices accordingly.

For example: In 1980, Michael Dell bought his first computer – an Apple II. In 1984, because of a $1,000 investment, Michael Dell became the Chairman and CEO of Dell Computer Corporation. By 1999, Dell Computer Corporation had become the number one computer company in the United States.

There's no way to give you the exact template to use that will guarantee you'll pick the best career path or be paid six figures, but to get additional career planning information, visit the websites listed at the end of the chapter.

". . . We must remember that intelligence is not enough. Intelligence Plus Character – That Is The Goal of True Education."
—Dr. Martin Luther King Jr.

Be Mindful

No matter what occupational arena you choose, you will need to prove your ability to handle challenges, demonstrate responsibility and initiative, learn from experience, motivate others, and achieve results.

No matter what your level of ambition, be aware of the knowledge and skills that will be valuable in the future – don't become outdated.

During the planning process and prior to making any career moves, always ask yourself the following questions:

1. What are you working for? Status? Wealth? Material comfort?

2. Do you want a family at some point? When?

3. Do you want to become a manager or just be a member of the team?

4. Do you want to own your own business (whether big or small)?

5. Do you want to remain in a particular geographical area? Will you relocate?

Mistakes

Many people think that if they look hard enough they will find their dream job. I'm of the belief that generally, dream jobs don't *already* exist. Most people that tell you they are working in their dream job have actually *created* the work or service they perform. Don't expect to find your dream job in the classified ads in Sunday's paper.

Everyone you share your dream with will not share your enthusiasm. They will steal your joy, and tell you that your dreams are unrealistic and unattainable. Remember, just because others don't see the big picture doesn't mean you still can't continue dream it.

If a job opportunity sounds too good to be true, it probably is. Especially if it requires you to invest money, relocate, or do something unethical. Con artists understand the passion people have for a great career (dream job) and they play and prey on that. Do your due diligence and research all aspects thoroughly.

Don't be so attached to your idea of the perfect career that you pass up opportunities that could turn out to be better than your current job and career path. Stay open to new ideas and concepts, but don't settle for something that doesn't fit your core or use your skills and talents.

Final Reminders

Serve – Do you only serve yourself? How can your talents best be used? What issues in business or the community do you care about? Do you ever wish you could change something or make a difference?

Dream – Think about a dream you have buried away because someone told you it wasn't practical or achievable. Dreams can come true, but first you have to be willing to dream them.

Joy – Do what brings you joy. When you do what pleases you, you will probably find that you are acquiring knowledge and skills.

Real – Make it real by writing it down. Write down the description of your dream job. The more detailed you are about what you want to do, the more opportunities will begin to appear. A realistic and achievable plan helps you gauge your progress.

Assess – Assess your current skill and talent levels. Gain clarity so that when opportunities emerge, you are able to make informed choices. Consider these questions:

• Which of your skills and talents are unused?

- What does your dream job look like?

- What are you willing to sacrifice to have your dream job?

Limits – It is easy to assume that you will occupy the same type of job forever. However, this can narrow your career possibilities dramatically. Don't limit yourself.

Flexibility – Overly detailed planning will leave you very little or no scope for responding to the changes in circumstances that will inevitably occur.

In an increasingly uncertain world, build your employability by accumulating skill and experience. While there is no hard and fast rule that will guarantee your success, the ultimate responsibility for acting (or reacting) to changing circumstances is yours. Remain true to yourself always, and reach for the stars!

Reading Resources:

For the most up-to-date information about financial aid supplied by the federal government, call the Federal Student Financial Aid Information Center toll-free at the U.S. Department of Education at 1-800-4FED-AID. You can also obtain a guide to federal financial aid for students, called The Student Guide, which provides an extensive and annually updated discussion of all federal student aid programs. You can obtain the Guide by writing to the following address:

Federal Student Aid Information Center
P.O. Box 84
Washington, DC 20044
Or call: 1-800-4FED-AID

For the latest Department of Education publications on topics related to going to college, call **1-877-4ED-PUBS toll-free,** or visit www.ed.gov/about/ordering.jsp.

Information on planning for college early can be found on the Department of Education's *Think College Early* web site, at www.ed.gov/offices/OPE/thinkcollege/early/.

www.collegeview.com

www.fafsa.ed.gov

www.fdncenter.org/

www.collegenet.com

www.collegeboard.org

www.careerbuilder.com

www.careerkey.org

www.princetonreview.com

ABOUT THE AUTHOR

ESTELLA RAYFORD

Estella Rayford is a retired Police Sergeant who majored in psychology and graduated from Wayne State University with a Bachelor of Science degree. She is a training coordinator and instructor, leadership and life coach, mentor, and personal trainer. When she is not training or mentoring someone, or taking another class, she is working out or researching another way to increase her investments.

She is also a member of the Professional Woman Network, the American Red Cross, Women of Wayne State University Alumni and several other associations. She resides in Detroit, Michigan.

Contact:
Estella Rayford
18986 Harlow
Detroit, Michigan 48235
(313) 532-4151
msbossiflossi@earthlink.net

THIRTEEN

MONEY MANAGEMENT

By Estella Rayford

Does this sound familiar? You are young, making money, and spending it faster than you can get it. You are not saving it or keeping enough to carry you over from week to week, or month to month. You run short of cash at least three days before you are paid, and cannot buy food, gas, or pay bills. That is because you are not controlling your money; your money is controlling you.

Money management, sounds like a chore doesn't it? It is something you may not even want to think about. But you need to because it is *your* money, and if you start managing *your* money now, it becomes less of a chore and more of a way of life. You probably think you have time to get started later, or that you do not make enough money to even think about money management. If you have money incoming on a regular basis, then it does not matter how much it is, you need to manage it. Instead of thinking that it is something you can't or don't want to do, think instead that it is what you *need* to do to keep up with your money, no matter how little or how much you have.

If you are still in college, money management could help in terms of having a small credit card debt or no credit card debt when you graduate. You will have a head start on how to manage your money when you start working and supporting yourself.

Here are just a few points involved in money management:

- Budgeting

- Saving

- Spending

- Insurance

The majority of young men in college, leaving college, or already in the work force do not have a clue about budgeting. Actually, before you can perform the other three well, you need to learn how to budget. You may or may not know it, but budgeting is a very important part of money management. It is the first thing you need to do to begin to manage your money. When you budget your money, you are keeping track of your incoming and outgoing expenses. You are making sure you know where your money is at all times.

Some people use a paper worksheet and some use a computer to help chart their budget. You can Google "money management" and check out some of the different sites to see if you can find a chart or worksheet that you think might work for you. One website that is very useful and geared toward young males and females and their money is: www.youngmoney.com/money_management.

Money Management Budget Worksheet (sample)

Monthly Income_____
Bi-Weekly Income_____
Weekly Income_____

	BUDGET FOR	ACTUAL SPENDING
Expenses		
Savings		
You (15%)		
Emergency funds		
Other (donation, vacation, etc)		
Food		
Groceries		
Lunches		
Meals out		
Housing		
Rent/Mortgage		
Utilities		
Insurance		
Taxes		
Clothing		
Work attire		

Leisure/sports		
Laundry/dry cleaning		
Health (medical, accident/disability)		
Insurance		
Medical, vision, & dental visits		
Automotive		
Car notes		
Car insurance		
Gas		
Maintenance/repairs		
Taxes		
Income taxes		
Totals		

Budgeting helps you control your problem expense areas. It also helps to see how much money you really have or do not have for spending, saving and insurance. Some experts say to prepare a yearly budget chart and review it monthly. But, if you are just getting started, I suggest you start out with a weekly, bi-weekly, or monthly worksheet first to see where your money is actually going. Then, you can see where to stop the outgoing **wants** of your expenses and start controlling the outgoing **needs** of your expenses much better.

Whether you are still in college, living at home, or have a place of your own, create a worksheet that works for you. You can add or eliminate areas as needed.

Adjustments may occur once you have established a budget to decrease outgoing expenses, giving you more money to use where needed, or to save. You will also be able to put more money into your emergency money savings account. In this ever-changing economy, you definitely need an emergency money savings account. You may not think that you will be able to save any money, but even if you are only able to save $25 per pay period, it is better than **nothing** saved. Try for 15% per paycheck. In order to be able to put money away for later, you have to stop living above your means. If you make $25,000.00 per year **after** taxes, live like you make only $20,000.00 **before** taxes. Don't frown; you can do it.

When you have a savings account, you have to make sure and check on it. If you have the money payroll deducted, then you will have the 15% portion on your budget plan already taken care of. Qualified plans (retirement accounts) are just some of the different savings accounts you could put your money into.

Qualified plans always have something to do with deferring taxes. In other words, instead of paying more taxes on your income now, you pay fewer taxes on the money you put into your savings to use for later when your income tax bracket is lower. A 401(k) is one of the qualified retirement savings plans offered by some employers. The employer usually matches the employee payroll contribution to the 401(k) to a certain amount. You can contribute up to $15,500 in salary deferrals, and your employer may make a matching contribution or profit sharing contribution up to 25% of compensation up to a maximum of $45,000 for 2007.

Traditional and Roth IRAs are two more qualified retirement savings accounts that you could utilize for your future. Both are retirement accounts that you could contribute to on your own. You can have more than one IRA retirement account open. The maximum limit you can contribute per year is $4,000, but in 2008 the maximum will rise to $5,000. This is a combined total for all of your IRAs. Before you decide on which one you want, make sure and do some research on them to help you decide. I recommend the Roth IRA if you are going to be opening an IRA account because, even though you cannot claim the contributions on your taxes now, you will not have to pay taxes later when the distributions start.

Mutual funds, bonds, and stocks are other ways to invest your savings to earn for the future. If you are interested in learning or trading knowledge about them, a good website to visit is www.stockgang.com. There is no dollar limit on contributions to your investments with these types of savings. With more money to save, you will be able to put more into your 401(k), Traditional IRA, Roth IRA, mutual funds, bonds, and the list goes on.

When you have decided on where to put the money you are saving, you have to check on it. You should always read your investment statements and any other type of savings statements that you get. You should also check on your money, even when a statement is not due. Statements may come monthly, quarterly, or annually. It just depends on what company you have chosen to do business with. You could get a financial advisor to help you with your investments, however, make certain that they are competent, and that they are looking out for *your* financial well-being (and not *their* financial well being) with your money. This is especially important if you are investing in mutual funds, stocks, and bonds apart from employer retirement accounts. This includes checking on your 401(k) and IRAs, too. The company and/or financial advisor may or may not be investing, handling your funds properly, or the way you may feel that they should be. In addition, financial advisors do charge a fee for their services. The bottom line is, it is your money, and if you save or invest, check on the status of your money. If you start saving and investing now, you could see your money grow to a substantial amount by the time you reach your 40's.

Go ahead, check the savings calculators. I found several different savings calculators online. If you check www.youngmoney.com/calculators, you will find calculators to use to calculate how much money you can have five, ten, fifteen, or more years from now, based on the amount you want to start with and how much you can put into your savings per month.

Keeping watch on your money may ensure earnings verses spending. The bottom line is money management. This brings me to my next point of money management, **spending**. Spending falls under money management because spending your money is one of the major reasons why you cannot save, pay your bills, or even support yourself.

When you open up a credit card account and start charging everything you want, do not think that you are not spending any money. You are, because if you do not pay the balance, you are paying for what you charged, and you are paying an extra 19% - 22% interest rate that the credit card company tacks onto your unpaid balance, just to use their card. If you have not done so already, **do not open a credit card account if you are** not **prepared to pay the balance every month**. If you do have a credit card already, or you have more than one, pay off the smaller card balance(s) first, and then pay more than the minimum on the card(s) with the larger balance(s) until it is paid off. Call the creditor to see if you can have the interest rate(s) lowered. Think about it, would you rather be paying the creditors 19% - 22% interest, or would you rather see your money earn you interest? That is just too much spending, and usually nothing to show for it except debt. If you own a debit card, you could also be spending your money even faster than usual, because it is easy to forget to record the time and reason you used your debit card, and before you know it, you are paying overdraft fees to your bank or credit union, and that means more debt.

If you stop to think about where your money is being spent, you probably cannot remember. If you do not keep a record of your spending, it will get out of control. Think about your management worksheet.

Remember the column for **food**? Groceries are a necessity, but buying your lunch everyday is not. Taking your lunch to work at least four days a week can eliminate that expense. Cut back on eating in restaurants and buying fast foods to once a week, or once every two weeks, instead of nearly every day. Buy your groceries with the intent of preparing your lunches for work or school and preparing your dinner every night. Cook enough for dinner so that you can take the leftovers for lunch the next day.

Let's talk about your living expenses. If you are renting an apartment or house where you have to pay for your own gas and electricity, you can lower your utility bills with a few adjustments. Just lower your heating temperature in the winter when you are gone for at least four hours or more, and raise your cooling temperature in the summer. Change your light bulbs to the more energy efficient bulbs. They cost more, but they last longer. Until you need to use them, unplug appliances that you are using infrequently or only once a day. Doing these things will help to lower your energy bill considerably, thus cutting back on spending and giving you more money where you need it. If your phone bill is costing you more than $1,800.00 a year, then you are paying too much, unless you can write the expense off on your taxes. You might not want to, but you need to seriously think about whether or not you really need all of the extras on your cell phone. Eliminating some of them could help lower your bill.

Do you like going to the movies? How often? Two or three times a week? Do you take a date, or that special someone? Do you purchase popcorn, candy, soda, nachos, and hotdogs? In addition to all of that, what about dinner later? One movie date could cost you as much as $50 or more. If you did this two or more times a week, it could run into a lot of spending. Think money management.

Ok, now what about that **car**? Do you think you need a car to go to and from work, school, or to go on a date? What kind of car do you drive, and what is your car note and car insurance expenditure? If you are driving an expensive car, trading it in for a less expensive one could save you a lot of money that you could be investing. A more expensive car or an SUV means more money spent on car notes, car insurance, gas, maintenance, repairs, and upkeep. Oh my, more spending. So, is having the expensive car or an SUV a good investment? It does not sound like it. Sounds more like poor money management. Does the value of the car go up every six months? No, it goes down! This means no gain. Buy a less expensive car and save the extra money that you will have from smaller car notes, lower car insurance, lower gas needs per month, and lower cost on maintenance, repairs and upkeep. This is good money management.

Young men already have to pay a higher insurance premium than women in their age group. The less you spend on a car note and insurance premiums, the more you have to save and invest. With the money you save from eliminating all of the excess spending, you could be building a sizable stash of money. Think about having a savings account as insurance for "what ifs". Remember, money management.

This brings me to the last point regarding money management, **insurance**. You are probably wondering what insurance has to do with money management. If you are paying unnecessarily high insurance premiums for your car, home, health, and life insurance, then that would be taking more money out of your pocket, and that is poor money management. You may think that the only insurance you need is car insurance if you have a car, but that just is not true. In fact, I know it is not true. There are several reasons and types of insurance you will need now and later in life. Having insurance for different reasons is just as important in money management as budgeting, saving and spending. You need car, homeowners or renters, health, (which covers many different types of insurance), and life insurance.

When you buy insurance, and you do need to buy insurance, make sure you do not go with the first one you see advertised. Check around, research, and ask your friends and family about theirs. Check for the cost and coverage.

Do not assume that because you are young that you do not need life or medical insurance. You are not going to live forever, and during your lifetime you may, or may not, need health assistance. Health insurance is used to indemnify the insured (that's you) against medical losses due to accidents, sickness or disability. Medical expense insurance, disability income insurance, and accidental death and dismemberment insurance are the three most important areas of health insurance.

Health insurance is available through individual or group policies. Check with the many different insurance companies and see what kind of health insurance coverage they offer for students and young people. Ask the insurance companies if they offer health insurance for young people at a lower premium rate. Do not think that because you are young and healthy, you do not need any health insurance. My son thought the same thing until he had to pay out of pocket for a doctor's visit, that was very expensive. Now he has health insurance. When you start looking for health insurance, make sure you understand what you want from the insurance company, and what it will cost you out of pocket. Learn what health insurance terminology means. You can go on the Internet and find some common terms to know at www. healthinsurance.org. This will help when you are ready to purchase some health insurance.

Find out if your vision and dental are covered; ask about the cost of out-of-pocket routine doctor visits. Ask about accident and disability coverage, in the event you are disabled and unable to work due to an accident or illness. These things are important, too. Sometimes it may cost you more, but the benefits of coverage are priceless if you have an unforeseen illness, accident, or disability.

Last, but not least, is **life insurance**. I know you are thinking, "I'm young, I don't need life insurance." Young people usually do not need life insurance; however, there may be a few reasons why you do need life insurance, although it is still your choice. I will say this; you do need some life insurance if there is someone in your life depending on your support. There are different types of life insurance. There is Term-Life Insurance, Whole-Life Insurance, and Universal Life. You do not have to buy, but at least check it out and know before you buy.

Manage your money for now and later. **Make sure you manage and control your money, and do not let your money manage and control you.** Respect yourself and respect your money. It is called money management.

ABOUT THE AUTHOR

Suzette C. Boyette

Suzette C. Boyette, ARNP is a mother of three, a UF Gator and practices as a Women's Health Nurse Practitioner (ARNP) at the Student Health Center at the University of Central Florida. She is also a Certified Childbirth Educator and a Certified Parent Educator.

Her passion for educating parents has evolved into the creation of Parents Everywhere, Inc., a new media company that specializes in education for parents. She and her husband, Troy hope to help parents become more effective all over the world through her classes, workshops and podcasts (Internet radio shows). To learn more, please visit their web site www. parentseverywhere.com. Listen. Learn. Give.

She also reaches families by volunteering monthly at the Greater Orlando Compassion Outreach Center and the Healthy Start Programs in Florida teaching parenting & newborn care classes; helps pregnant teens at the Beta Center; and teaches others in organizations such as the Girls Scout Citrus Council and Head Start Programs.

She is also a professional member of Attachment Parenting International, a partner in both the 4C Head Start Program and Healthy Start Program, a certified member of both the International Network for Children and Families (INCAF) and the Childbirth and Postpartum Professional Association (CAPPA), the National Association of Women's Health Nurse Practitioners, the East Orlando Chamber of Commerce, the eWomen Network, the YaYa Network, and the National Association of Women Business Owners.

She is a motivating and energetic speaker who will present to any group interested in learning about parenting and family health. Having presented to numerous moms groups, preschools, elementary schools, church organizations, PTA meetings, hospitals and other groups of teachers and/or parents throughout Orlando, Suzette has learned to easily engage her audience and her enthusiasm is contagious. In July 2008 she will be a speaker for one of the sessions at the 6th Annual Ya-Ya Networking Conference.

She also has started to pursue her passion for writing. She has a regular column, Ask Suzette in an Orlando parenting magazine and is also a contributing author of this book.

Contact:
Suzette C. Boyette
1969 S. Alafaya Trail #185
Orlando, FL 32828
(877) 980-2828
sboyette@parentseverywhere.com
www.parentseverywhere.com

FOURTEEN

MAKING A DIFFERENCE: VOLUNTEERING

By Suzette Boyette

Hurricane Katrina. This powerful force of Nature changed the lives of thousands and also mine. Even now, years later, the vivid images of pure devastation is still clear in my mind. The despair behind the eyes of everyone, the look of utter hopelessness, was something that spoke to my soul. Here I was in my safe little world. I was blessed with good health, a wonderful family, beautiful children, a supportive husband, and a warm home. And there on the cold screen of my television were fathers, mothers, and children without even the bare necessities. Children... I have three little ones of my own. I felt this sudden, unfamiliar need - almost like I needed air. I needed to do something to give back. But, how could I with three young children? What could I do to possibly change the life of someone in my own community that needed it? I thought that maybe I could give them clothing, a warm meal, a shoulder to lean on - just something.

That something was one simple word that had so much power: **Volunteer**. It's an action word and a noun. *I* can volunteer. *You* can volunteer. *All of us* can *volunteer*. The beautiful thing is that all it takes is *one* person. Volunteering gives you the opportunity to change people's lives, including your own. Helping others has become such a significant aspect of our lives in America that high schools now require students to complete a certain number of community service hours or volunteer hours before they graduate. This may sound challenging and even frightening, but if you follow these easy steps, you will be able to design your future, and discover a whole new world opening up just for you.

How Do I Start?

If you want to help solve a community problem, work towards a worthy cause. To grow as a person, volunteering has a great deal of benefits in exchange for your gift of time and expertise. Organizations such as United Way, Girls Scouts, and Kids Health offer various steps to help you decide where you want to volunteer.

Step 1: Ask yourself what your interests are. Volunteering can help you to explore what you are really interested in. Find out what's right for you.

- If you like animals, you can help at your local animal shelter or veterinarian's office. You may also call your local zoo, theme park, or animal sanctuary for opportunities.

- If you enjoy working with children, you may volunteer at a preschool program, summer camp, after-school program, or be a mentor for children at a school. You may also call upon homeless shelters for children, hospitals, and community outreach programs that work with children.

- If you like sports, call and visit your local YMCA, Boys & Girls Club, and area schools. Also, do not forget to contact the local sports leagues, such as Little League or soccer.

- If you like to cook, gather some of your closest friends and family members and make a meal for a soup kitchen or a homeless shelter. They would so appreciate a home cooked meal.

- If you like working with the elderly, call your nursing homes, hospitals, and meal service programs, such as Meals on Wheels.

- If you like sewing, you may sew some clothes or bedspreads for a local women's shelter, or sew some robes or pillows for a nursing home. There are some organizations that sew for a cause.

- If you like the outdoors, you can volunteer by clearing/cleaning a neighborhood park, plant some flowers for a nursing home or neighbor, mow yards, or build something, such as for Habitat for Humanity.

- If you have more than one thing you love, you can try to combine your interests. For example, if you love sports and children, consider volunteering at a local YMCA and be a volunteer coach for the soccer team.

Action Point: On a separate sheet of paper, write down as many things you can think of that you are interested in. Then, narrow it down to the top five things you like to do or are interested in and write them here:

1. _____

2. _____

3. _____

4. _____

5. _____

Once you've identified or narrowed down your interests, you have a myriad of resources to help you in your quest of finding a place to volunteer.

- One of the greatest resources you have is looking online. Use the Internet (use any of the search engines such as Google) and type in what you are interested in and the name of your city.

- You can also type in the word "volunteer" and research the various categories listed.

- You can ask your teachers, counselors, sports coaches, ministers, your neighbors and your friends. Use the members within your own community and ask for their help in identifying the right organization to fit your interests. You will be surprised at the network of people you already have!

- Last, but not least, do not forget your own family. They will not only help you, but they will also admire and applaud your genuine desire to help your community. Who knows? They may even go a step further and volunteer WITH you. What wonderful memories you will make together as a family!

   Action Point: Write down the five resources you can ask for help:

1. _____

2. _____

3. _____

4. _____

5. _____

1. <u>Volunteering can help you to learn about possible careers for your future.</u>

- If you are interested in the medical field, you can volunteer at a hospital in their newborn nursery, pediatric floor, or any of the medical floors. You may also visit a retirement or nursing home and learn the medical aspects of their care.

- If you are interested in teaching, you can volunteer for any of the after-school programs to help the children with their homework, or you can tutor a student. You may also become a mentor for a younger child, or volunteer to be a teacher's assistant in his/her classroom.

- If you are interested in science, try volunteering at a museum, greenhouse, laboratory, or if you are fortunate to live in Cocoa Beach, Florida or Houston, Texas, you can try to volunteer at the Kennedy Space Center.

- If you are interested in the performing arts, work with the artists or actors at your local community theaters, dinner theaters, or university theater programs.

- If you are interested in office or clerical work, call up any non-profit organization, church office, or small business and do their filing or front desk duties.

2. <u>When you volunteer, you may meet people you may not ordinarily meet.</u>

- If your grandparents have passed, you can volunteer at a nursing or retirement community, and you can become friends with an elderly person and have them be your "adoptive grandmother."

- By volunteering at an agency that works with people with mental or physical challenges, you will learn the beauty of life, and how similar they are to you, despite these differences.

- If you volunteer at a sports complex, you may meet the coaches of some famous sports figures, or meet the people behind these admired men and women.

3. <u>By volunteering, your volunteer activities look good on college applications and work resumes.</u>

- When colleges look at applications, they want to see that you are a well-rounded individual who looks at the world around them, and is genuinely interested in contributing to their community. They want to know you as a person, not as a list of high SAT scores or straight A's.

- Potential employers want to see that you have made a commitment and stayed with the project or organization. You've made it on time to the appointments, are responsible, and can get along with others. Also, the different groups you have volunteered with may provide your potential employers with excellent references.

- Volunteering shows schools and employers that you are willing to sacrifice your time and energy to make the world a better place.

4. <u>It is fun to volunteer, and it makes you feel good.</u>

- Giving your time and of yourself makes you feel good about yourself, and boosts your self-esteem.

- This is a great way for you to get a perspective on your own life, and allows you to focus on others and away from the problems in your life. You immediately see that your involvement in the world is meaningful.

- By working with others for a period of time, you begin to develop lasting friendships.

- Others who volunteer often say that they receive far more than they had anticipated. The experience is so satisfying and rewarding... more than words can say.

Step 2: Okay, I've discovered what I'm interested in and where I want to volunteer. But, how much time do I need to devote as a volunteer?

Do you think you need a lot of time to volunteer? Or, do you think that you are TOO BUSY to even start to think about volunteering time you don't have? If you answered yes to both questions, then no wonder you haven't taken the first steps.

Volunteering takes as much time as you can give. If you are able to give one hour a week, congratulations! How lucky are you to be able to give that time and for those you are helping. Not too many people have that luxury, especially if you have a full-time job, or are a student. If you are only able to give one weekend a month, or even only one day every six months or even less a year, you can still find some way to volunteer, and your time is welcomed. Find what fits into your schedule. A fantastic organization, United Way, encourages volunteers to organize their thoughts of time in these categories. So, if you can give **one hour**, you could:

- Give blood.

- Register to vote.

- Donate old clothes.

- Gather non-perishable foods and take them to your local food pantry.

- Buy a small item to donate to a child.

- Read a book to a group of children at the hospital, children's shelter or library.

Or you could:

- Spend time with patients/elderly at the hospital or nursing home.

- Serve meals at a homeless shelter.

- Pick up trash at a local park.

- Help care for animals at a local animal shelter.

- Tutor a child after school.

If you can give a **weekend,** you could:

- Help build a home for Habitat For Humanity.

- Get involved with a community clean-up effort.

- Create murals at a local children's center.

- Participate with a community event or fundraiser, such as a walkathon.

If you can give **one hour a week**, you could:

- Be a coach for a child's sports team.

- Be a mentor for a little boy or girl with the Boys & Girls Club.

- Be a tutor for a child at the YMCA or local school.

- Visit a lonely elderly client at the nursing/retirement community.

- Deliver meals to the elderly through Meals-On-Wheels.

Action Point: Determine how much time you are willing to give. Then, write down five ways you could volunteer, based on the amount of time you are able to give:

1. _____

2. _____

3. _____

4. _____

5. _____

Step 3: I'm almost totally convinced that I should volunteer. What are some of the other benefits of volunteering?

There was a study done by the Natural Survey of Giving, Volunteering and Participating in 2000. Here is what they found:

• More than three quarters (79%) of volunteers said that volunteer activities helped them with interpersonal skills, such as motivating others, understanding people better, and dealing with others, especially if they had challenging and difficult personalities.

• Just over two thirds (68%) said that they learned how to communicate better. 63% stated that they increased their knowledge in the particular area of interest they were volunteering in, such as health, politics, women or the environment.

• *More than half of the unemployed volunteers (54%) believed that by volunteering, they would increase their chances in obtaining a job*

Making A Difference: Volunteering 187

Another study conducted by the Corporation for National & Community Service in 2006 found the following health benefits of volunteering:

- Volunteering leads to greater life satisfaction and lower rates of depression.

- Volunteering and physical well-being are part of a positive reinforcing cycle.

- The best way to prevent poor health is to volunteer.

- People who volunteer live longer.

It all makes sense, doesn't it?! If you give back to your community, you feel good. You feel like you are making a difference in the lives of others, as well as for yourself. You develop a healthy sense of self, strengthen you self-confidence, and become more positive. Your self-esteem is skyrocketing, your spirit it full of life, and you laugh more often because you are having fun and doing what you are interested in. And more importantly, doing what you enjoy! So, of course, you are healthier!!! It's a no brainer, right?

Volunteering = Positive Self-Esteem = Good Health

It's the circle of giving. It really has no beginning and no end. What comes around, goes around. All good things happen to the volunteer and those receiving the gifts from volunteering.

To review what we've discussed, here are a few tips to remember:

- Be selective about where you volunteer.

- Choose carefully.

- Research the causes that are important to you.

- Consider the skills you have to offer.

- Learn something new

- Don't over-commit your schedule.

- Consider volunteering as a family.

Step 4: So, now that you've decided on where you want to volunteer, now what?

You have to contact the organization and do a little more research to make sure it is where you want to devote your gift of time. Here are a couple of suggestions.

1. When you call an organization to volunteer your time, be sure to ask for the volunteer coordinator. Be ready to answer some of the questions they may ask you:

    - Why do you want to volunteer with our organization?

    - How many hours would you like to volunteer per week/ per month?

    - When would you like to volunteer?

- Do you have any special skills?

- Do you have any special interests?

Making A Difference: Volunteering 189

- Do you have transportation?

- What do you know about our organization?

2. Remember, when you are speaking to the volunteer coordinator, feel free to ask them questions, as well. You are also interviewing them to make sure you really do want to volunteer with this particular organization.

   - What is your expectation of volunteers?

   - What kind of training will I receive?

   - How many hours do you expect me to volunteer?

   - How many other volunteers do you have?

Step 5: Where Can You Go to Volunteer?

If you need just a little more help, here is a list of places you should consider giving your gift of time and energy:

- Meals On Wheels

- Habitat for Humanity

- State Parks

- City Programs

- Hospitals

- Libraries

- Nursing Homes/Senior Citizen Centers

- Food Banks

- Ronald McDonald House

- YMCA

- Special Olympics

- Animal Shelters

- United Way

- Girls & Boys Club

- Girls Scouts

- Boys Scouts

- Red Cross

- Salvation Army

- Goodwill

- Churches

Action Point: Pick three to five places that you like and give them a call. You will find the one for you, and they will thank you for choosing them!

1. _____

2. _____

3. _____

Making A Difference: Volunteering 191

4. _____

5. _____

Will you take that first step in making a difference in your life… in your future?

Believe me when I tell you that volunteering will change your life in ways you never imagined. Your heart will take on a mind of it's own, and you will have this light inside you that others will be drawn to. It's a ripple effect. You touch the life of one person, and that person touches the life of another, and that person touches the life of another. You get the picture, yet? Just by helping one person, *YOU* affect the lives of so many people! How cool is that?!

You will meet wonderful people who are just like you. You will learn how gracious and beautiful the lives of others are when you connect and share yourself. You will be overwhelmed at the goodness that *truly is* in our world, but unfortunately never knew existed. Doors will open. Your heart will shine. Your future will be what *you* design it to be. *You have that power.*

Young man, the question I have for you is, "Are *you* man enough to design *your future* for yourself, or are you going to have *others* design it *for you?*"

Trust yourself. Trust your heart. And you will see that **you do make a difference.**

Notes:

ABOUT THE AUTHOR

PATRICIA FAULK DUNCAN

Patricia Faulk Duncan is CEO/Managing Member of Wonderland Support Services, L.L.C. Wonderland put families and small businesses under the protection of some of the best law firms across North America; Protect and Restore their Identity for a small monthly fee. In addition Wonderland provides Networking Opportunities, Education and Resources for Women and Small Businesses.

Mrs. Duncan secured an Associate of Science degree in Nursing from Macon State College in Macon, GA, a Bachelors of Science degree in Nursing from Georgia College & State University in Milledgeville, GA, and an Executive Masters of Business Administration from Wesleyan College in Macon, GA. She has traveled and studied International Business in Moscow and Ulyanovsk, RUSSIA.

Patricia Duncan is a Registered Nurse, Licensed Nursing Home Administrator, Certified Paralegal and an Independent Associate/Group Benefit Specialist with Pre-Paid Legal Services, Inc. She is a member of PWN , 2008 International Advisory Board Member for the Professional Woman Network, Macon Exchange Club, Think Pink Committee of the Internationally Award Winning Macon Cherry Blossom Festival, NAFE, National Notary Association, and is a Nafe Network Director for the Women on the GO Network.

Mrs. Duncan was the recipient of the 2007 23rd Annual Leadership and Courage Award presented by Dr. Harry Ross and rossreportnews.net.

Patricia Duncan provides motivational trainings, workshops and keynote speaking for youth and women in churches, schools, corporations and the long-term care industry.

She founded the A&M Book Club in July 2007 in memory of her grandmother Mrs. Alice Jackson and Mrs. Mattie Turner and has been featured in the Georgia Informer August 2005 and the Ed Grisamore Column of the Macon Telegraph August 2007.

She resides in Macon Georgia with her very supportive husband Paul Sr., inspiring son, Paul Jr., daughter Genetra and 2 sets of twin granddaughters.

Contact:
Wonderland Support Services, L.L.C.
3780 Napier Avenue
Macon, Georgia 31204
(478) 474-5519 or (478) 731-8761
www.wonderlandsupport.com
wonderland3780@yahoo.com
pat1656@bellsouth.net

FIFTEEN

NO HEALTH! NO WEALTH!

By Patricia Duncan

"Look to your health, and if you have it, praise God, and value it next to good conscience; for health is the second blessing that we mortals are capable of; a blessing that money cannot buy."—Izaak Walton

As a teenager, you go through numerous changes. Your body is on its way to becoming the size of an adult. You may have noticed that the size eight shoe that you wore last month no longer fits! You are probably becoming more independent and making more choices on your own. Have you been told by your parents, teachers, pastors, friends, etc. about "making choices" about your life? Some of the greatest choices you will face are about your health!

What is health? According to Webster Dictionary, health is physical and mental well-being; freedom from disease. Now what is Webster's definition of wealth? Wealth is much money or property; riches. In order to gain wealth, you must be healthy, graduate from high school, go to college or technical school, and then the sky is the limit! **Your**

health is a big factor in this goal! Employers seek individuals that are prompt, dependable and productive. Being healthy will make you able to meet these goals!

As a mother of a 13-year-old son, a cardiac nurse, and an entrepreneur, I want to take a short time and talk to you about some of the biggest choices you will face. It took me nine years as a nurse to realize what having good health really means. I had a young mother on my hospital floor that had two sons, ages 10 and 12. She had been diagnosed with serious heart problems. She and I had a long conversation about her health, and how she wanted to see her sons graduate from college. As I was exiting her door, she said to me, "Patricia, take care of yourself. Without health, there is no wealth." This conversation has played in my mind many times. It was not very long after her hospital stay that this mother died.

Now that you know that I am a cardiac nurse, please let me tell you about some disturbing issues that I am seeing with young men. I have seen young men as young as 30 years of age having open-heart surgeries. I feel compelled to talk with you briefly about this scary thought. **Yes, teenagers can have heart attacks**! Any severe chest pain should not be dismissed. Report it to your parents, coaches, teachers, or a responsible adult immediately!

According to the April issue of JAMA, obesity continues to be a leading public health concern in the United States. Overweight prevalence tripled in children and adolescents aged 6 to 19 years.

Now, whether this obesity is due to sedentary lifestyles (lack of exercise), genetics (passed down from parents), or nutrition, it can lead to some serious health problems. The main health problems are heart attacks, strokes and diabetes. There was a study in the recent issue of *Pediatrics* that included an article by two cardiologists from the Heart

Center at Akron Children's Hospital about <u>heart attacks in nine healthy teenagers</u>, eight of whom were male. These teens were all 12 to 20 years old. They had no obvious risk factors and normal coronary arteries. This is just a reminder that we all can help prevent heart attacks by avoiding cigarettes, not being overweight, controlling diabetes, eating plenty of fruits and vegetables, and exercising daily. We will discuss these same points later in the chapter.

We have been discussing, thus far, your physical health. All of your body, mental health, emotional health, and spiritual health play a big part of your physical overall condition. Being mentally healthy makes you realize your own ability to cope with the normal stresses of life. This allows you to work productively, then being able to make a contribution to your community. Being emotionally healthy makes you in control of your thoughts, feelings and behaviors. You feel good about yourself, and have good relationships with your family, neighbors and peers. Being spiritually healthy is the way you find meaning, hope, comfort, and inner peace in your life. Some find spirituality through religion, music, art, or a connection with nature. The mind, the relationships, environment and spirituality all have a part in maintaining your health and treatment of diseases.

What are you doing to take control of your health?

1. _____

2. _____

3. _____

Are you athletic, musically inclined, or computer savvy? What successful individual footsteps would you like to follow?

My idol_____

Now, if I were to pose this question to my son, his answer would be Michael Jordan. As you already know, Michael Jordan, by acclamation, is the greatest basketball player of all time. Michael Jordan had power and speed! Maybe you are a NASCAR racing fan, so your idol might be Richard Petty, nicknamed "The King" of NASCAR Racing. What about Walter Payton, nicknamed "Sweetness", one of the greatest NFL running backs to ever win a Super Bowl Championship? Let us not leave out Bill Gates, one of the best-known entrepreneurs of the personal computer industry, and one of the richest men in the world!

As you and I know, all of these individuals are successful in their own way. I can tell you that, in order for them to make all those accomplishments, they had to make a decision early in life to take control of their health. I can also bet that these individuals developed healthy habits, including eating nutritiously and being physically active, to help them feel good, and look good on the field, track, court, etc. Well, there are lots of reasons you should care about your health, like feeling good and getting stronger, doing well in school, at work, in sports and other activities. Believe it or not, these can all be affected by your health!

Why should I care about my health? List four reasons:

1. _____

2. _____

3. _____

4. _____

Now, I don't know the game of football like my husband and son. My husband has coached Little League football for eight years. He literally eats, drinks and sleeps football! Because of my husband and son, I attend the games, watch football on TV, and dream about it!

Taking care of your health is like an intense game of football! It is a crucial part of your life.

You've got to prepare yourself to win! **Let's Play Some Football!**

Your health is the football; you want to get it into the end zone. Okay, we know if you get it into the end zone, you are in the scoring zone. The score of the game is 6-6. So let me go over the **six** points of a healthy life with you:

1. **Eat well-balanced meals. This should include:**

   • **Fat:** avoid eating too much

   • **Milk:** 2-3 servings per day (Milk, yogurt and cheese are great!) *Growing bones and teeth need lots of calcium, especially during this time in your life when the rate of bone growth is high!*

- **Meat:** 2-3 servings per day
  2 tablespoons of peanut butter count as one ounce of meat!

- **Vegetables:** 3-5 servings
  A great source of vitamins and minerals!

- **Fruit:** 2-4 servings per day
  A great source of vitamins, carbohydrates and fiber!

- **Bread** 6-11 servings per day
  A great source of carbohydrates, vitamin B and Iron!

- Drink 6-8 glasses of **water** daily.

- Take a **multi-vitamin** daily (as prescribed by your doctor).

- Remember, **breakfast** is the most important meal of the day!

How can you change your eating habits to well-balanced meals?

_____

_____

_____

2. Be Smart. Don't Smoke!

Every cigarette you smoke takes away seven minutes of your life. Smoking causes cancer, which can lead to death and many other health problems. What will you do when your friend offers you a cigarette? What will you do to stop smoking?

_____

_____

_____

3. Exercise as much as possible daily.

- *Walk or ride a bike to see friends (with parent's permission).*

- *Take a 10-minute break (jog in place, stretch, etc.) while reading, doing homework, searching the web, or watching TV.*

- *Take the stairs rather than the elevator!*

How will you incorporate exercise into your daily routine?

_____

_____

_____

4. Stay away from Alcohol!

Alcohol is like a sedative (soothes, quiets); it depresses your brain and slows down its ability to control your body and mind. Too much alcohol can lower your breathing and heart rate to a dangerously low level, or even STOP IT! What will you do if offered a drink? What will you do to stop?

_____

_____

_____

5. Say "NO" to Drugs!

You control what happens; by taking drugs, they take control of your mind. How will you say no to drugs?

_____

_____

_____

6. Think before having Unprotected SEX!

Before having unprotected sex, ask yourself: Is this someone that I want to spend the rest of my life with? Is this person worth dying for? Having unprotected sex one time can cause you your life. Remember, if a child is born, this person will always be in your life. Once having unprotected sex, you are having sex with everyone that she has had sex with. (Not to mention if HIV or AIDS is contracted, it can lead to your DEATH!) Are you ready for the consequences of unprotected sex? If NO, why?

_____

_____

_____

Imagine that these six points are tackles in your life, and not blocking yourself against them will put you on the ground face down every time!

Now remember that this is an intense game. It is the 4th quarter, and there are 12 seconds left. The clock is running. This is a crucial time in your life. It is Do or Die Time! It is the 4th and Goal. It is your last opportunity to get to the end zone of health and wealth! It's huddle time; you get into your huddle to re-evaluate your life and what you must do to WIN! In the huddle, several things must take place:

1. Remember, you've already conditioned yourself to win: physically, mentally, emotionally and spiritually.

2. You must understand why you are striving to win, and know your reward is a long, healthy and wealthy life!

3. You must encourage yourself on a daily basis by associating with positive, influential and honest people.

4. You must stay in the fight, even if you only have 12 seconds to change your health!

5. Finally, you've got to give it all you've got!

Now that you are doing whatever it takes to have a healthy life, you are blocking and advancing to the end zone of Health and Wealth! You get into the end zone, YOU SCORE! You win the game! **The score is now 12-6!**

Now is the time to take charge of your health. Making even small changes for the better will help you to look and feel great!

P.S. The best resources for health information advice, and if you need treatment, are your parents and your doctor.

"Even a child is known by his doings, whether his work be pure, and whether it be right." —Proverbs 20:11

Exercise:

To be smart with your health and score a touch down, list what you're going to do:

Steps:

_____

_____

_____

_____

_____

Remember, no health - no wealth!

Notes:

ABOUT THE AUTHOR

CHARLES MICHAEL "MIKE" COLEMAN

Michael Coleman holds a Master of Business Administration from the University of Indianapolis, and Bachelor of Science Degree in Political Science from Western Illinois University. He is a Regional Human Resource Manager for Belk Department Stores Inc.and has been involved in retail management, training, and human resources for more than 25 years.

Mike Coleman is President and Founder of the Mike Coleman Institute, a resource organization dedicated to improving the professional, personal, and family life of men. Michael is a member of the National Fatherhood Initiative (NFI). The mission of NFI is *"To improve the well-being of children by increasing the proportion of children growing up with involved, responsible, and committed fathers."*

In 2002, Mike attended a seminar offered by the Professional Woman Network (PWN) and the information presented was so powerful he decided to join PWN. Mike has used the unique perspectives and insights gained from PWN to better understand the dynamics between men and women.

Mr. Coleman is a PWN certified trainer in professional presentation skills, women's wellness, and diversity issues. He has offered programs on family wellness, teen development, and workplace diversity. Inspired by the work of PWN and NFI, Michael is developing **retaildad.com** a resource network for men in the retail industry.

Currently living in Dallas, Texas with his family, Mike is a devoted husband, and father of two boys. He is an active member of Grace Outreach Church in Plano, Texas.

He would like to dedicate this book to his family Robin, Joshua, and Conner. *Thanks for laughing with me on the good days, and loving me through the difficult days.*

Contact:
Retaildad
Box 237
4760 Preston Road, Ste 244
Frisco, TX 75034
mikec@retaildad.com
www.retaildad.com
www.protrain.net

SIXTEEN

ASSERTIVENESS VS. AGGRESSIVENESS

By Mike Coleman

Marcus slammed his fist through the kitchen wall, then turns to his mother screaming, "You just don't get it... I have to go to the dance. You can't stop me!" Before his Mom, Barbara can utter a word, Marcus crashes out the door to join the guys from the basketball team.

Barbara stands in the middle of the floor staring at the fist sized hole in the wall. She is dazed and confused. With tears streaming down her face, and her hands shaking she tries to collect herself. She recalls that just 2 days ago Marcus said he did not want to go to the party. Barbara wonders what went wrong.

Assertiveness vs. Aggressiveness

One of life's tougher challenges for men is communicating feelings in a assertive way. Most teenage boys struggle to understand how to express themselves clearly, and are either unassertive (passive)or overassertive (aggressive). Not understanding how regulate aggression leads to frustration and misplaced emotions. In this Chapter we will, explore assertiveness, aggressiveness, and how to use each behavior effectively.

Assertiveness

Assertiveness is expressing your ideas or opinions in an open, honest way that does not violate the rights of others. Assertiveness is also taking a position that may be different from everyone else, maintaining that position while respecting the rights of other people to disagree. Assertiveness does not mean allowing your ideas or rights to be restricted by another person or situation.

Aggressiveness is assertiveness on steroids. Aggressive behavior violates another person's rights, personal property, and boundaries. The primary focus of an aggressive person is to dominate others to gain their own way. Aggressive people often use violence to get their way. Name-calling, ridicule, public humiliation, threats, taunting, gossip, finger pointing, and sarcasm are some other tactics used by aggressive people. People get aggressive when they stop being assertive. Often times, the aggressive person is simply afraid or uncomfortable.

The Right to Assert

The first step on the road to assertiveness is recognizing that you have a right to be assertive. Yet, as with all rights, there are obligations that must be honored. Assertiveness is only possible when all the people involved understand and accept that each person has rights.

- You have the right to state your own ideas and feelings.

- You have the right to say no, without feeling guilty.

- You have the right to choose your friends.

- You have the right to not join a group or gang.

- You have the right to make a mistake

- You have the right to feel good about yourself.

- You have the right to not be perfect.

- You have the right to ask for help; and not feel bad for doing so.

- You have the right to be frustrated.

- You have the right to be quiet.

- You have the right to tell other people how you want to be treated.

- You have the right to be heard and to be taken seriously.

Assertive Communication Skills

It can be scary to tell people how you feel. One reason it's so hard is because you may not know exactly what you're feelings are. Unfortunately, there is no magic formula to explain feelings or emotions. Still, you must try. Here are a few communication techniques that may be helpful:

- Do not violate the personal space of the person you are speaking to.

- Maintain eye contact with the people you are communicating with.

- Use a respectful tone of voice.

- Remain calm.

- Stay focused.

- Start your statements with "I".

    o "I need you to…"

    o "I will not…"

    o "I don't understand."

- Be direct, and give the message to the person it is intended for. If you have a problem with Jake, don't discuss it with Bill.

Assertiveness and Happiness

Practicing assertiveness does not mean life will be easy. You will not always get what you want. In many cases, your attempt to be assertive will be met with hostility and aggression. Your parents may tell you that you're being a jerk for stating your position—*keep trying!* Friends will laugh at you when you make a decision for yourself, and not for them--*don't give up!* Girls may call you a loser because you decide that they are not the best person to be in your life—*believe in yourself!* Being assertive could lead to the loss of a close friend or relative—*keep walking!* The best way to become assertive is through practice. Effective assertiveness is like learning to ride a bike; the first couple of times are awkward. You may fall down and scrape your knees, but you keep trying to ride. As you become better at assertiveness, you can expect some positive life changes:

- Increase your self-esteem

- Improve your decision making skills

- Improve your leadership skills

- Improve your self-confidence

Passiveness

When you allow the views, beliefs, concerns of others to become more important than your own, you are being passive. Passive behavior is dishonest because it hides your true feelings. When you keep your feelings hidden, it tears you up on the inside. The built-up pain comes out in other emotions like fear, anger, and frustration. It might seem easier to put your feelings on the inside rather than confront a difficult situation. But, nothing could be more dangerous to your emotional development. Passiveness can be dangerous because it keeps you from becoming a strong man.

Remember the story of Marcus? Let's see what is going on in his life now.

Two hours later at the party, Marcus is feeling guilty about what happened. He is wondering what his Mom is doing. He doesn't know why he got so mad at her. She was just talking to him, and he exploded. Marcus can't understand why he hit the wall; he's never done that before.

Earlier in the week, Marcus told his Mom did not want him to go to the party because the older guys on the team were mean. But, for some reason when the guys invited him to the party, he was afraid to tell them no. Rather than express his true feelings assertively, he responded passively by saying "why not". Marcus is feeling bad because he was not honest with his teammates or friends. He is feeling guilty for the way he treated his Mother. **Assertiveness only works when you are honest with your feelings, and you consider the rights of others.**

Selfishness

Unfortunately, many people will view your need to be assertive as selfish. If you act reckless and disrespectful towards other people, you're being selfish. Selfish behavior often gets met with an aggressive, sometimes violent response. Parents, teachers and other concerned adults will usually react to selfish behavior with an even greater amount of force. They see your behavior as something that needs to be controlled.

Aggressiveness

The intention of aggressive people is to control other people so that they may have their own way. When you act aggressively, it can quickly destroy any respect that people have for you. You may get your way in that situation, but the victory comes at a great cost. Moreover, the people that you have hurt could become vengeful or seek to retaliate. Even worse, they may never forgive you. Think of the aggressive words you have heard or used, "You'd better...", "Keep it up!", "You're going to get it!"

Social Aggression

One of the most painful times in a teenager's life is having to go through the constant teasing and attacks from other boys. There is a strong desire among some boys to show their masculinity by attacking a weaker boy. The attacks usually start around the age of 12, and will continue to the age of 16. After age 16, the intensity of the attacks decreases. Unfortunately, some boys continue the behavior well into adulthood.

Social scientists tell us the reason for the aggression can be found in the animal behavior known as the *"pecking order"*. Among chickens, the most powerful bird can peck on any other bird in the flock. The second most powerful bird must show respect for the dominant bird, but may peck on all the other birds in the flock. Another example can be seen in wild dogs. Dogs will fight and battle until a ranking order is established in the pack. The weakest dog must be submissive to all dogs in the pack.

Humans "pecking order" flows from parents to children. The parents discipline the children; the oldest child will discipline or peck the younger sibling. The youngest sibling, in turn, will peck on the family pet. Boys, more than girls, like to peck or pound on objects. I still have great memories of taking a hammer and smashing concrete blocks until I made little rocks.

From early in childhood, boys understand that being a man is determined by how masculine you are. Unfortunately, the government has not given us a standardized test for determining masculinity. Unlike teenage girls, who identify puberty with their first period, teenage boys do not have one single life-defining event. So, like all the other games we learn as children, when there are no rules, someone comes up with one, and the contest begins.

In most cases, athleticism or verbal cruelty are the barometers used to determine masculinity. In this system, the only way to gain status among your peers is to be bigger, meaner, or stronger. You are constantly subjected to teasing, insults, and intimidation. The emotional pain of the attacks is devastating; often times lingering into adulthood.

Another reason for the constant attacks is because your body is changing. In puberty, the changes are both dramatic and erratic. Often times, the dominant boy at age 12 will be the average boy at age 16.

The Bully

What sets bullying apart from other types of conflicts is the imbalance of power. The goal of the bully is to make someone a victim. The bully has no regard for the rights of the person they are attacking. Bullying is an intense aggression that involves one boy using threats, insults, intimidation, or physical force against another boy. Bullying can also be a group against one boy, or a group of boys against another group of boys. While bullying can involve physical force, the most common type is verbal. Spreading rumors, teasing, name-calling, are just a few tactics of choice for the bully.

If you are being bullied, it is important that you tell your parent, teacher, coach or clergy. I know the thought of facing a bully is scary, but please **DO NOT SUFFER IN SILENCE**. If you do nothing, the bullies will continue to torment you. The bully and his gang want you to think that if you tell an adult, you're being a snitch. The fact is, their power comes from keeping you silent.

A Note to the Parents and Concerned Adults

Thank You!

If you are reading this far into the chapter, it means that you are committed to a young man's success. You are also well aware that being a teenage boy is not easy. During this time, it is normal for the boy to seek independence from the family. The young man needs your love, support, and understanding now, more than ever.

- Boundaries are important; they need to be clearly defined.

- You should expect him to test the rules.

- Keep the lines of communication open.

- Work with him to be assertive; respect his need to assert.

- When he makes a mistake, respond from a position of love.

- His view of the world will seem to conflict with your core values.

- He will develop friendships that you may not like.

- Some of his reckless and defiant behavior will push your patience to the limit.

Recommended Resources:

Raising Cain - Protecting the Emotional Life of Boys by Dan Kindlon, PhD & Michael Thompson, PhD

The Young Woman's Guide for Personal Success - For Teenage Girls and The People Who Love Them. Edited by Linda Ellis Eastman

http://www.fatherhood.org/

http://www.boysproject.net/index.html

ABOUT THE AUTHOR

KARLENE EWING

I WOULD LIKE TO DEDICATE THIS CHAPTER TO MY GRANDSON, John Scott Bailey, who has just graduated from high school and will be entering college to begin a career for his future.

"You have to do your own growing no matter how tall your grandfather was".............*Abraham Lincoln*

"One is taught by experience to put a premium on those few people who can appreciate you for what you are"...............*Gail Godwin*

"Wisdom is knowing when to speak your mind and when to mind your speech"...unknown

Karlene Ewing serves on the international Senior Advisory Board for the Professional Woman Network, and is a member of the Professional Woman Speakers Bureau and the Author's Speaker Bureau. Ms. Ewing's career in Human Resources includes having served as Director of Human Resources for several healthcare facilities, Corporate Human Resources Director, and Director of a Surgery Center. She has been involved in several start-up programs and hospital mergers. In 2000 she started her own consulting business, KE Consulting, which has been primarily focused on healthcare facilities. In this chapter, she speaks with much authority, having interviewed several thousand applicants over the past twenty years, and developing extensive experience in employee investigations. Ms. Ewing is also co-author of *"Becoming the Professional Woman," "A Woman's Survival Guide for Obstacles, Transition and Change"* and *"You're on Stage! Image, Etiquette, Branding & Style."*

Contact:
KE Consulting
5145 W. Goshen Avenue, #228
Visalia, CA 93291
559-623-9788
Kewing100@aol.com
Kewing100@comcast.net
www.protrain.net

SEVENTEEN

GETTING THE JOB AND KEEPING IT

By Karlene Ewing

Choosing a career path will be one of the major factors affecting your life. Successful accomplishment can be made easier by beginning to prepare yourself **NOW.** This chapter will guide you through the process of choosing a career, preparing yourself, interviewing, and ultimately getting the job and keeping it.

You will also learn the importance of appropriate interviewing etiquette and appearance, including information on grooming.

Preparing For Your Future

- What do you enjoy doing that would have value in the business world?

- What is your passion?

- Can you make a living by following your own interests or hobbies?

- Believe in yourself and your abilities (talents).

- Don't put yourself down.

- Build your confidence by volunteering in community and church activities.

- Develop an honest value system and conscience. Our conscience gives us integrity. Listen to that still small voice inside you.

- Personality Tests help you define a career that fits you, and also provides a guide for the type of personalities you can work with the best.

- Understand your personal value.

- Develop good "word habits." Using such words as "I just…" or "I'm sorry, but…" preceding a statement diminishes the value or force of what you say, and expresses a negative attitude.

- Volunteer. Be active in your church and community. Volunteer activities will prove to be as valuable on your future resume as "paid" work, and can also be a guide to help you decide on the type of work you enjoy and get the most satisfaction from.

Design an Eye-Catching Resume.

Prepare a concise, easy-to-read resume that clearly defines your education, past experience (both volunteer and employment), community involvement, and future goals. Make sure there are no misspelled words, and use proper grammar and sentence structure.

References can be listed on a separate sheet of paper, or simply state at the end of your resume that "References will be supplied upon request." Put your name, address, and telephone number at the top of the first page, as well as any other contact information, such as fax, cell phone, and e-mail address.

If you are mailing the resume, it must be accompanied with a short (typed) letter that clearly defines the position that you are interested in being considered for. Sign the letter above your typed name at the end of the letter. Place the resume and letter (**do not fold**) in a large envelop. If you are responding to an advertisement, be sure to state this in the cover letter. Example: I am submitting my resume to be considered for _____ position which was in the (name of paper, magazine) on (date). Be sure to follow all directions that are requested for submitting your resume.

If you do not hear from the company, feel free to follow up with a short letter or telephone call stating when you sent your resume, and emphasize your interest in working for their company.

One Resume Does Not Fit All.

- A common mistake many people make is to use the same resume for numerous positions.

- The resume will be the first step in the job selection process, and if it does not spark an interest in the reader, the process will end there.

- Design the resume to fit the position and the company.

Interviewing Etiquette and Appearance:

<u>**The definition of interview**</u> – "A formal consultation, usually to evaluate qualifications. A meeting at which information is obtained."

<u>**The definition of etiquette**</u> – "The conduct or procedure required by good breeding or prescribed by authority to be observed in social or official life." "Personal conduct or behavior as evaluated by an accepted standard of appropriateness for a social or professional setting."

<u>**The definition of appearance**</u> – "External show." Attitude, behavior, demeanor, manner, poise, posture.

It is essential that you establish a professional rapport with the interviewer from the very first moment that you meet. Be honest, sincere, and genuinely grateful for this opportunity. It isn't necessary to say it in "words", but show it in the way you respond and interact with the interviewer, the company, and the position.

- Look the interviewer in the eye and smile.

- Extend your right hand for a firm (not limp) sincere handshake. If there is a reason that you must shake with your left hand, you might say, "Excuse my left handshake," so they are aware that you know the proper etiquette for shaking hands.

- Do not sit until you have been directed to do so.

- Do not sit with your leg crossed over the knees.

- Place your hands in your lap in a relaxed manner.

Be Prepared.

Research the company, and be prepared to speak and/or ask intelligent questions. Good research sources are 1) Chamber of

Commerce (local and state) 2) Better Business Bureau 3) Library 4) Internet.

What to research:

1. Name of Company

2. Location of Company

3. Are they a stand-alone, parent, or subsidiary?

4. What is their product or customer base?

5. How long have they been in business?

6. How many employees do they have?

• Gain as much knowledge about the position as you can, which will be valuable in asking appropriate questions.

• Know the correct spelling and pronunciation of the interviewer's name.

• Know the interviewer's correct title (call the receptionist to obtain this information).

• Bring paper, pen, and a copy of your resume.

• Be punctual.

Prepare yourself by answering the following questions, and then study your answers until you are comfortable with them. Have a friend ask you these questions…not once, but several times. Practice in front of a mirror.

Review! Review! Review before your interview!

Exercise:

1. What is your strongest asset?

_____

_____

_____

2. What is your greatest weakness?

_____

_____

_____

3. What type of supervision do you work best with? i.e., lots of direct supervision, minimal

_____

_____

_____

4. Tell me about a conflict that you had with a co-worker or supervisor and how you handled it.

_____

_____

_____

5. Would you handle it differently now? If yes, how?

_____

_____

_____

6. What life accomplishments are you most proud of?

_____

_____

_____

7. Why should you be considered for this position? Please don't say, "Because I need a job."

_____

_____

_____

8. Are you a team player, or do you prefer to work alone?

_____

_____

_____

Suggested Proper Clothing Guidelines

Dress shirts tend to shrink, so it would be a good idea to purchase a sleeve that is slightly longer than normal for you.

- Your sleeve should cover your wrist and reach to the beginning of your thumbs.

- Cuffs should be tight enough to prevent slipping down from the wrist.

- If you prefer to wear your button-down shirt on the outside of your pants, it should hang just above your pants zipper and/or back pocket level.

- When you are wearing a jacket, extend your arms, and the sleeve should fall between ½ to 1 inch past the jacket sleeve.

- Shirt seams should meet the shoulder.

- Forefingers should be able to fit in between your collar and your neck when the shirt is buttoned at the top.

- Collar tips and outer edges should be covered by your blazer or suit jacket lapels.

Jacket/Blazer

Your jacket or blazer sleeve should rest at your thumb knuckle when arm is extended. The jacket should cover your backside.

- The collar should leave ½ inch of dress shirt's collar visible.

- If you plan to wear your sports jacket over a sweater, then take one with you when trying on a jacket or blazer.

Pants

Khaki and dress pants should end at top of heel, and should not reveal sock as you walk, or show more than 2 inches of sock when you are seated. Jeans can fall at the bottom of the heel.

Important Do's and Don'ts for Presenting Yourself for a Proper Confident Interview:

- Carry a brief case or messenger bag, never a backpack.

- Do not wear too much cologne and do not mix scents.

- Funky facial hair – it is better to stick to a mustache or beard neatly trimmed.

- Use special trimmers for nose and ear hair.

- Ties – choose classic width of 3-1/2 inches and make sure pattern and color compliment your shirt.

- Clothing should neither be too tight nor baggy.

- Do not wear excessive jewelry. Do wear a simple watch and a wedding band and/or class ring.

- If you wear a ponytail, it should be neat and clean, and not fall past base of neck.

Prepare Your Internal and External Self for a Confident Interview.

Your internal self will reflect externally. What makes up your internal self?

- **Self-Esteem** – A confidence and satisfaction in oneself

- **Confidence** – Faith and Trust. *A feeling or consciousness of one's powers, or of reliance on one's circumstances. Confidence stresses faith in oneself and one's powers without suggestion of conceit or arrogance.*

- **Self-Pride** –

  ○ Pride – *the quality or state of being proud. A reasonable or justifiable self-respect. Delight or elation arising from some act, possession, or relationship.*

  ○ Self-Pride – *a pride in oneself, or in that which relates to oneself.*

- **Positive Thinking and Speaking** – *fully assured; influence for good; uplifting; not negative.*

- **A Good Value System Guided by Your Conscience** – *the sense or consciousness of the moral goodness or blameworthiness of one's own conduct, intentions, or character, together with a feeling of obligation to do right or be good.*

You are probably wondering how all this can affect your interview. The interviewer will be able to "read" your inner self quite well. He or she is trained to do so. Consider the following when understanding how important your attitude will be during the interview. Prepare your inner self in the following ways:

1. Look at life with a positive attitude, and approach negotiations with an attitude that allows both parties to win. You will then be more effective at eliciting cooperation, and ultimately getting what you want.

2. You must be deeply fascinated by the life of every person, customer, employee, and colleague that your life touches. You must be deeply grateful for who they are and what they do. If you develop a sincere love, you will automatically be fascinated with and grateful for them. This is your inner-self, which reflects your outer-self.

3. If you are fascinated with those around you and you discover how to value their lives, and if you are *genuinely grateful* for their patronage, partnership, and friendship, you will show them in ways that are sincere and meaningful.

These are the essential elements of a fabulously productive person/ relationship, which is reflected by your ***inner-self***.

The Interview Language

The three languages of an interview are (1) body (2) verbal (3) appearance. All are equally important.

Body Language

- Sit back in your chair.

- Do not slouch.

- Keep your hands comfortably in your lap.

- Avoid twiddling your thumbs or making quick sudden movements.

- Sit with legs crossed at the ankles, or together with feet on the floor.

- Look attentively at the interviewer, but don't stare and do not continually look down, as if embarrassed.

Verbal Language

During the interview, the interviewer will be evaluating how you communicate verbally, as well as what you say.

- Practice using good English, which not only means the words you select, but also the grammar. "I don't have any," instead of "I don't got any."

- Speak positively rather than negatively, or in an apologetic manner.

- Know the language of the position and the company.

Appearance

You want to be neat and professionally groomed, but not overdressed for the position or the company.

- Check your appearance in a full-length mirror. Is your clothing neat and clean? Are your colors coordinated? Are your shoes polished and clean?

- Are your fingernails clean?

- Is your hair clean, good hair cut, and appropriately combed?

The Interview

Arrive a few minutes early (never late). Announce your name clearly to the receptionist, and state the name of the person you have an appointment with. Do not say that you are there for an interview, as it may not be common knowledge that a position is open. Be courteous and friendly, but do not engage in flirtatious chit-chat, which is not professional conduct.

- Never take another person to the interview with you.

- Take a deep breath and relax.

- Don't chew gum or suck on mints.

- Make sure your breath smells clean and fresh.

- Don't put your sunglasses on your head.

- Be personable, listen carefully, and show interest.

- Do not interrupt the interviewer.

- Be comfortable with silence. Don't become nervous and feel you have to speak just to fill the silence.

- Be honest. It is better to say, "I do not know" or ask for clarification, than to make up an answer or respond with incorrect information about your experience.

- Don't trash the company's competitors or other applicants. This shows insecurity on your part, and that you probably would not be a good team player.

- Don't put yourself down. If you have received praise for work you have done, admit it, but don't boast about it.

Concluding the Interview

The interviewer is the one who concludes the interview, not the interviewee. I was interviewing a very good candidate until she said, "Is that all? I need to go." Needless to say, she did not get the job.

- You will probably be asked if you have any other questions or comments regarding the job. If there are none that you can think of, don't just say "no." Rather, express your appreciation for the time spent with you in explaining the position and the company's policies.

- Tell the interviewer that you are interested in the job (if you are), and that you look forward to hearing from the company.

- After the interview, send a hand-written note to the interviewer expressing your appreciation for the interview, and stating your interest in the position.

- If you do not hear from the company in ten days, it would be appropriate to follow up with a telephone call.

Good luck with your next interview! Using good etiquette and being professionally attired will open many doors for you.

Keeping the Job

Companies are looking for employees who are capable, willing, and enthusiastic about being a part of a team to advance the future goals of the company.

- Be flexible and willing to learn and follow the routines in the job.

- Be a team player, not a loner only interested in advancing your own agenda.

- Show your dependability by being punctual and doing your best in all that you are asked to do…and more.

- Do not get caught up in gossip and jealously, which is destructive to everyone and cannot help you perform to your best level.

- Always be honest and straightforward.

- If you make a mistake, admit it.

- If you don't understand something, ask for help or clarification.

Make Yourself Valuable to the Company.

- Volunteer for special assignments.

- Learn as many functions of the company as you can.

- Join professional and community organizations and participate actively in them.

- Take classes and advance your knowledge and skills.

Work each day, treating each project as though it is a stepping-stone to your future. Think before reacting and don't burn your bridges. You never know who is watching you. Don't hold a grudge against fellow workers.

If you follow the steps outlined in this chapter and believe in yourself, there is no limit to the success you can achieve.

Recommended Reading:
Radical Edge by Steve Farber

ABOUT THE AUTHOR

ROSEMARY MEDEL

A City Planner for the last seventeen years in Southern California, Rosemary has worked for the cities of Huntington Beach, Cypress and Signal Hill. A Bachelor of Fine Arts degree with an emphasis in Environmental Design, California State University at Fullerton has prepared Ms. Medel for her current profession in Land Use Planning. She feels strongly about giving back to her community and has volunteered her Planning expertise to the community where she currently resides. Rosemary is a former Planning Commissioner for the City of La Habra where she assisted in guiding development during her three-year term. Currently, Rosemary is a Realtor, and is the owner and president of The Medel Group. Her firm is committed to training and preparing its clients facing risks with confidence, develop their professional image through improved public speaking and presentation skills. She is a co-author of *You're on Stage! Image, Etiquette, Branding & Style, Emotional Wellness for Women: Mind Body & Spirit, Survival Guide for Overcoming Obstacles, Transition & Change, Women as Leaders, Beyond the Body! Developing Inner Beauty,* and *Young Man's Guide for Personal Success.* She is slated to author the future book *The Baby Boomers Handbook for Women.*

Rosemary is a certified trainer in Woman's Issues and a certified Professional Coach and is an International Advisory Board member of the Professional Woman Network. She is also a member of both The Professional Woman Network International Speakers Bureau and the National Association of Female Executives. Rosemary is available for personal and professional coaching sessions.

Her most important role and accomplishment has been raising her two grown children Rosalie and Eli.

Contact:
Rosemary Medel
The Medel Group
P.O. Box 2204
La Habra, CA 90632-2204
rosemedel@juno.com
www.TheMedelGroup.com

EIGHTEEN

OVERCOMING HURT AND SADNESS

By Rosemary Medel

I am waiting on the tarmac at Phoenix International Airport preparing to travel to Kentucky and a sense of peace comes over me. Not long ago there was little peace to be found recalling the turmoil in Eli's life. You see, my son Eli was going through his first heartbreak. This was not the heartbreak of a teenager, but rather that of a young man who had invested time, effort, and more importantly his heart into his first serious relationship.

Let me give you some insight into Eli's character. When he was two years of age, I was decorating his room with gifts he had received from the holidays and his birthday. And I placed a lamp designed with a stuffed bear that played music. Although I do not recall the song, what was touching was when I turned the key to play the music and I felt small arms hug my leg and Eli began to weep as the music played. I picked him up and asked, "What is wrong son?" And through his tears he said, "The song is too sad." Needless to say, the lamp was removed immediately. Eli is still that sensitive caring person he was years ago.

The impact the serious relationship breakup had on him was heartbreaking to his family, as we saw his pain and knew this was his lesson to experience, but that we could offer loving support. The ex-girl friend had no vehicle for over six months during this year long relationship. Eli would take her to and from work each day. They both worked in the same place, which made it a little easier. He loved her and was happy to help her. In my observation, he was a great boyfriend.

What was not revealed to me until the breakup commenced was that she would sometimes invite Eli to her home, often to discover she was not there or would make other arrangements with a girlfriend. While most adults would end the relationship merely on that behavior, young people are much more tolerant because of their innocence and lack of experience to know when you are being taken advantage of. (Having raised a daughter as well as my son, I have seen both sides of relationships and the dating process from the perspective of a parent.) So, from the view of young people, I surmised that girls think guys are dogs and boys think that girls are only interested in guys who treated them badly! Some things just don't change! I believed everyone just wanted to be treated with love and respect! This is a simple concept right? WRONG! Now breaking up is not straightforward. It is done with a more non-committed method called "Taking A Break"!

Eli and me at my daughter Rosalie's wedding (taken before the breakup)

Taking a Break

I know Eli's story is not unique. Can you relate to this experience, as well? When this breakup process started, Eli told me that they were on a break. What the heck is taking a BREAK? What are the rules for taking a break? This is a term unfamiliar to me as used today. Last time I heard this term, it was from an episode of "Friends" when Rachel and Ross were on a break. No one could agree on the terms of the break! I was told that it means you are not seeing each other as boyfriend or girlfriend. I was also informed that it is today's kinder way of breaking up. This I disagree with.

What does taking a BREAK mean to you?

_____

_____

_____

_____

_____

Do you agree with this method of ending a relationship? _____
If not why?_____

_____

What would you change?_____

_____

A 'My Space' Breakup

Communication among young people today is all revealed as instant online news. The Internet allows information to be shared instantly regarding current relationships, past encounters, and who your favorite friends are with the stroke of a few keys. While customizing your 'My Space' page, you select your music, background, video and favorite pictures. This seems like an expression of individually, but it is also revealing to the world your true character. Now, let me give you a different scenario. Let us say that you both agree to take a break, but then you go to her 'My Space' page and there it is like a slap in the face, her pictures have been changed on her page. She is now out partying with her friends and another guy.

How do you deal with that pain and hurt now? _____

_____

_____

The Internet is a tough place to go through hurt and humiliation. You see, there are several things that are happening here. First, you are dealing with major hurt and perhaps even betrayal. But, you have several choices, as well. You can confront her, leave a message on her page, or you can realize it is time to move on.

So, how is discretion practiced on your My Space page while perhaps your ex-girl friend may start to update her friend's list and in changing out pictures, which all of a sudden deletes YOU.

You must stay strong, knowing that you are a person of integrity. Do not allow emotion to begin showing the ugly part of breaking up. Remember that any negative expression towards your ex-girlfriend will demonstrate that she is still in control of *your* emotions. Does the Internet provide a place for insensitivity and disconnect with the human experience of emotions and breakups? Only you can answer this question.

Acceptance: It's Over

Accepting that it is truly over is always the hardest part of breaking up. For the one who broke up with you it may be easier, but you are left with all the questions. YOU are left with all the self-doubt. You may be asking yourself the following questions:

- Could I have done something different to make her love me?

- If I could have just helped her with her family problems, we would have been fine.

- If her friends liked me more, maybe she would not have broken up with me.

- If I were different, she would not have left ME.

Do you see how easy it is to put the blame on yourself? If relationships were only so easy, there would be fewer breakups. The truth is that the issues that made your ex so unhappy were most likely there before you arrived. Yet, it is when we are in relationships that all the STUFF shows up! YOU are only responsible for your happiness. This means that you take responsibility and are accountable for only *your* actions. Subsequently, if someone is treating you badly, then it is up to you to respect yourself enough and speak up. However, this means that there will be some heartache in the process.

What always hurts most is to realize that WE cannot heal the wounds of another unless they allow us to. You see, you are only in control of your own emotions. What you offer someone in a relationship is the love and honesty you bring. The risk is that you never know when it will no longer be welcomed.

Do not lose yourself in the process. Do not allow heartbreak to make you bitter and cynical. Now, what do you do with all your time? You need to get back in the game of planning your life!

Planning a Future

Finding yourself in the mist of turmoil is challenging. Do not lose hope. If you are an athlete, play your sport to help yourself deal with the physical stress of breaking up. With all the emotions and hurt of a breakup, you need to realize it takes a toll on your body and mind. Here is a list to start your healing.

- If you are a runner, RUN! This is a good way to center yourself and ease your mind.

- Play pick-up games of basketball.

- Join a sports league to keep yourself busy and interacting with people.

- Call your friends to just hangout and talk.

- Enjoy nature, take a walk.

- Get out the snowboard and hit the slopes.

- Ride for miles on your bike.

- Go fishing.

Stay close to your support system, as well. Let us create a list of who is your support system. Name them here:

- Parents: _____

- Friends: _____

- Teachers: _____

- Clergy: _____

- Family Members: _____

- Siblings/Cousins: _____

Eli is an athlete, and working out was a great help for him dealing with his pain. He also turned to his creative side to heal. You can be creative, as well. Here is a list to start you thinking of your interests:

- If you are a musician, play your instrument and perfect your skill.

- If you are a writer or prefer to express yourself in writing, then put pen to paper.

- If you are a lyrist, write.

- If you sing, let the voice express itself!

- Start a new hobby!

- Get your mind off the ex-girl friend.

Healing from hurt is not an easy process, so allow yourself time to grieve the loss. Allow yourself to cry as your soul heals, then open your heart to new possibilities, when you are ready. There are plenty of girls out there who would love to meet someone like you. **But you cannot**

move on until you let go of the hurt and sadness. Turn inwardly to get in touch with your spiritual side; maybe prayer is in order. Give yourself TIME to take care of yourself. Approach life with an open mind and open heart, never holding on too tight to anything or anyone. In relationships, both people have to want to be in the relationship. You cannot buy someone's love, as it is the only thing in life that must be **given freely.**

When Eli was going through this breakup, his close friends Danny, Jeff and Sean were there for him. They kept him busy with activities and just hanging out talking. Turn to your friends. Be kind to your family during your breakup, as they love you more than anyone and only want to see you happy. (We tend to lash out at those closest to us.)

Let us go over a final list to start the healing process to over come hurt and sadness.

• Be honest with whether you want to breakup or not.

• Live an accountable life: Be responsible for your actions.

• Let yourself cry.

• Live with dignity by avoiding Internet drama about the breakup.

• Make plans for your life while enjoying your friends.

Understand that the pain of breaking up will not last forever. You have loved before, and you will love again. Grieve the loss, feel the pain, and move on with your life.

Eli is fortunate to have a great support team. His sister Rosalie is one of his biggest fans. This chapter is dedicated to my son Eli, who faced hurt and sadness head on, took its best shot, and came out STRONGER! I am proud of you, son.

*Eli and
my daughter Rosalie*

ABOUT THE AUTHOR

DEANNE GREENE-BOOKER, CPS, PhD

Deanne Greene-Booker, PhD. is a Senior Human Resources professional, trainer and personal/professional mentor. She is a dynamic speaker and motivator who inspire individuals to reach their full potential. Deanne has a B.S. in Business Management, Masters in Human Resources Development, and is currently awaiting the conferment of her Doctorate in Business Philosophy from Capella University. She is also a certified professional speaker.

Because her entire career focus involves youth and people empowerment, she has dedicated herself to volunteerism as a community advocate – most recently serving in an advisory role in the development of a faith-based community youth facility. Additionally, she facilitates parenting and teen empowerment workshops for a local community non-profit.

Deanne is currently exploring several philanthropic business interests, which would enable her to donate her time and talents as an image consultant to promote empowerment and workforce readiness for teens, young adults and transitioning first-time offenders'.

Special thanks to her husband Derrick, son and stepdaughter, Robert and Alante', parents Junior and Rose Greene and sister Theresa Kearse for all their continued love, support and encouragement.

Contact:
Deanne Booker, CPS, PhD
1224 Rhodes Walk
Conyers, Georgia 30094
DeanneGreene@Netscape.Net
(770) 483-7483

NINETEEN

SPEAKING WITH AUTHORITY: THE POWER OF WORDS

By Deanne G. Booker

"Your word is a lamp to guide my feet and a light for my path."
—Psalms 119:105 NLT

Have you ever found yourself speaking negatively about yourself, your circumstances, or possibly thoughts of mediocrity? If so, it's time to learn the power of speaking positively about yourself and your future! Always remember, the sky's is the limit! The power of words has potential to elevate or deflate your destiny – and it starts with changing negative self-talk habits and developing positive self-talk techniques and affirmations. Today, you'll read about the importance of taking authority over your words, and how doing it positively impacts your ability to achieve your goals!

"Words are like seeds! When words are spoken, they get planted in our hearts, and whether they take root and grow is totally up to us. The way those words become reality is what we constantly dwell on. In other words, what you meditate on is what you're watering and what will manifest in your life." —**Joel Osteen Ministries**

By controlling your internal dialogue, or "self-talk," you begin to assert control over every dimension of your life. Moreover, when you see things optimistically and speak positively, you take authority over your circumstances. By doing so, you will elevate your self-worth and tenaciously give yourself positive reinforcement, recognition and motivation for a purpose-driven life.

Below are guidelines to help you develop your ability to speak with authority, and develop fundamental tools of positive self-talk and affirmative statements to live an abundant life:

- Personalize statements by using "I", not generic or broad terms.

- Keep affirmations short, positive and memorable. Refrain from using negative words, replace with only positive declarations. For example, "I will not be discouraged by negative statements of other people." Rather, say, "I am self-assured, worthy, and will always strive to do my very best."

- Keep emotion positive. An expression that produces a positive emotion reinforces the affirmation. An example, "My plan for an abundant life excites me."

- Declare affirmation in factual terms. Speak (with authority) the affirmation into existence, even if it's not yet achieved. The power of words shapes your future and fuels your subconscious to make them a reality.

- Affirm your goals frequently, not for approval, but to keep you motivated and fuel your subconscious to achieve your goals.

Since achieving your goals and quality of life are directly fueled by your subconscious, the most important element to keep you focused must be linked to mental activities to enhance awareness of anything contrary to reaching your goals. The impact of positive self-talk and affirmative statements is essential to achieving success in every area of your life. Below are some examples:

- I am worthy and capable.

- I can make a difference.

- I have unique talents and abilities.

- My future is bright, exciting, and has limitless potential.

- I am willing to take risks to grow and challenge myself.

- I am self-assured, worthy, and will always strive to do my very best.

In addition to these powerful tools of positive self-talk techniques and affirmations, see below for ten (10) critical supporting steps to realizing your goals:

- Get a mentor.

- Believe in yourself and enjoy life!

- Visualize achieving your goals – seeing it with your "mind eye".

- Write your goals (vision) clearly and realistically.

- Give yourself affirmations to remind yourself that you're capable and worthy.

- Change self-limiting statements to questions. Example: "I can't handle this" should be stated in question form – "How can I handle this?" In this way, you challenge yourself to think and grow.

- Celebrate small successes and view potential failures as opportunities to learn.

- Don't be afraid to make mistakes; don't punish yourself for making them; and, never give up!

- If you fail to plan, you plan to fail (author unknown).

- Be passionate about your goals, and never sacrifice it for monetary gain. Passion yields an inexhaustible source of resilience to attaining that goal.

There is extensive scholarly research that supports the theory that specific, written goals increase your odds of success, which is defined by The Merriam-Webster Dictionary as, "a favored or desired outcome as a result of effort" or the "attainment of a proposed goal." In short, when goals are written, it strengthens your commitment and keeps you focused to make them happen. In this way, there's clear direction and a plan to get there. Consider written goals as your map to fulfilling your life long dreams! As quoted by Ben Stein, "The indispensable first step to getting the things you want out of life is this: decide what you want."

Let's get focused and practice! Use what you've learned regarding the importance of speaking with authority, using positive self-talk techniques/affirmations, and the essential steps necessary in realizing your goals.

First, we'll start with an assessment of your personal interest(s). This assessment tool will assist you with taking a closer look at yourself as a person, and help you make informed decisions about your future. It is followed by a five year plan to outline and examine your personal goals by listing specifically what they are, thinking from a short-term to long-term perspective.

Exercise – Personal Interest Questionnaire (complete the following statements):

1. My best qualities are: _____

    _____

2. Two things I would like to change (or develop) about myself: _____

    _____

3. I am happiest when I'm: _____

    _____

4. I prefer not to perform the following tasks:

    a. _____

    b. _____

    c. _____

		True or	False: (check one)

5. I like working in a group setting. _____ _____

6. My preference is to work alone. _____ _____

7. I like working with my hands. _____ _____

8. I love to travel (road warrior work). _____ _____

9. I enjoy speaking (facilitating) in large groups. _____ _____

10. I like to "crunch" mathematical equations. _____ _____

Consider goals as stepping-stones that advance you from one place to another place. These stepping-stones can be small, large, far apart or close together. If you set the stones too large or too far apart, the chances of reaching your goal are considerably less; therefore, the keys are to celebrate small success on your journey towards achieving your goals, establish smaller milestones leading in the direction of larger goals, and set deadlines to keep you focused.

Exercise – Now that you've identified several of your personal characteristics, please use the above list to help guide your efforts to develop five personal goals, both short and long-term:

<u>1 year:</u>
1. _____ Achieve by: _____
2. _____ Achieve by: _____

Now, list two resources or actions needed to reach the above two goals:

a. _____

b. _____

3 years:

3. _____ Achieve by: _____

4. _____ Achieve by: _____

Now, list two resources or actions needed to reach the above two goals:

a. _____

b. _____

5 years:

5. _____ Achieve by: _____

Now, list two resources or actions needed to reach the above goal:

a. _____

b. _____

Remember, speaking positively and affirming your goals are the first two stages of realizing your purposeful dreams. Let's practice some more! Now, write down ten affirmations that will help you realize and stay focused on your previously written future goals to shape your future for success. Remember to keep affirmations short, positive and memorable. Refrain from using negative words, and replace with only positive declarations.

Exercise - List five affirmations that will help you realize your future goals and shape your future:

_____

_____

_____

_____

_____

Since you have an idea now of how your thoughts and feelings determine your actions, you must remember the importance of keeping your words and thoughts positive. In this way, you will automatically be a more focused-driven person and move more rapidly toward successfully achieving your goals.

In all this, one thing to remember is that it's virtually impossible to develop and grow to become successful without adversity, tribulation, and negativism of others. So, embrace difficulty as a learning experience, and look into the situation to uncover the positive and speak your desired outcome into existence! As a commitment to yourself, complete the below goal-focused pledge as a reminder of your commitment to realizing your purpose-driven goals:

My Personal Pledge:
I, _(insert name)__ , make the commitment on (__insert date____) to stay focused on my future goals, and remain positive in my approach. I will create a plan for achieving my goals, and stay focused on realizing my full potential. Ultimately, my goal is to become _____
_____. Today, I will create a plan to realize my ultimate dream.
Several mini-goals I will achieve on my journey towards my purpose-drive goal are:

1. _____

2. _____

3. _____

4. _____

Barriers to my success, real and imagined, I will overcome to realize my purpose-driven goals are:

1. To overcome ____(barrier #1 – describe it)_____ and ____(barrier #2 – describe it)_____; I will stop _____ and _____; Additionally, my prayer is_____ _____, with supporting biblical scriptures of _____ and _____.

I will partner with my friend __(insert friend name)_____ to check in on my progress every week/month/quarter (choose one) and hold me accountable. This is my personal pledge to the future I know I deserve!

Signature

Author's Notes:

You can make positive self-talk work for you in realizing your full potential! When you habitually speak to yourself positively, it has a very profound impact on your self-image. It fuels your ambition as well as eventual success; therefore, constantly think about the person you want to become, and stay focused on your future and your goals!

When things go wrong, look doubtful or appear too hard, respond positively by saying to yourself, "I believe in myself and my ability to overcome any situation in my life, and I'm excited about my future." Resolve to never give up, and remain positive in every situation. Resist all temptation to respond negatively – under no circumstances! View disappointment and setbacks as opportunities for growth, and speak to yourself optimistically – utilizing positive self-affirmations. Nothing can stop you from being successful when you keep your (positive) words and mental pictures consistent with your goals!

Words to ponder, according to Vince Lombardi, "Winning is a habit. Unfortunately losing is, too." – Choose to Win!

Notes:

_____

_____

_____

_____

_____

_____

_____

_____

_____

_____

_____

_____

_____

_____

_____

_____

_____

_____

_____

_____

_____

_____

ABOUT THE AUTHOR

LaSonya McPherson Berry

LaSonya McPherson Berry is an entrepreneur, trainer, consultant and personal/professional mentor. She is a dynamic speaker and motivator who inspires individuals to reach their potential. LaSonya has a B.S. in Industrial Engineering, Masters in Human Resource Development, and will complete her doctorate in 2008. She has obtained certification in Leadership, Personal Development, Diversity and is a certified Youth Trainer.

Prior to starting McPherson, Berry & Associates, Inc., LaSonya began her career as a counselor. She became a charter member of Jasper County Teen Peer Counselors. She was trained to counsel in areas of teen pregnancy, drug abuse, peer pressure and all adolescent situations. LaSonya worked with the Department of Social Services with their teen pregnancy program, and facilitated workshops with teenagers who were a product of generational mothers of teen pregnancy.

LaSonya understands the need for community involvement. She is an alumna of the United Ways' Volunteer Involvement Program that provides board training. Her community involvement and training resulted in a director position for Operation Dignity's Bankhead Courts Human Resource Center. The center offered training classes that were parallel to the Welfare to Work Program and that is what inspired LaSonya to start GET POISED, a training and development business designed to help people reach their destiny. She obtained additional training, certification and became affiliated with The Professional Woman Network, an international training organization, as an International Advisory Board member and trainer. The business was later expanded and became McPherson, Berry & Associates, Inc. She currently serves as president. She is a co-author of *Becoming the Professional Woman* in the PWN library.

Contact:
McPherson Berry & Assoc.
P.O. Box 260669
Decatur, GA. 30036
(800) 325-5269
www.mcphersonberry.com
www.mbableu.com
www.getpoised.com
lasonya@mcphersonberryassoc.com
www.protrain.net

TWENTY

THE FRONT OF THE PACK: LEADERSHIP SKILLS

By LaSonya Berry

Welcome to one of the most difficult positions to be in…. being a man. You will be responsible for your life, leading your family, possible career leader, and the main provider. In many cultures, the male holds a dominant role. You hold one, too! You are the dominant and ultimate leader of YOU! Either you will lead yourself, or give yourself for others to guide you. Leadership is about persuading, inspiring, motivating, and overseeing. In this chapter, you will be provided with leadership principles and skill development opportunities that will help you be in the front of the pack and poised for position.

When you achieve success in sports or any competitive activities, you are awarded with a trophy. I believe the same kind of award is available to everyone who achieves life success. Get poised for life success and you, too, can be a winner with a personal life-like trophy called "You". Others can see it all the time you are in their presence, in a picture, or when others discuss your success. It is more than the jeans you wear, the number of girlfriends you have, or the kind of ride you drive. So how do you get there? At the base of the Get POISED® trophy, there are three platforms representing the support of your image. At the very bottom level is one labeled "Spirit", then "Mind", and the next is "Body". They can help you to lead in such a way that you stand out to be the unique man of interest that you are. All of this helps you to lead others. You have to get the influence before you get others to follow.

Spirit

The spirit has been defined by dictionary.com as the principle of conscious life; the vital principle in humans; a divine, inspiring, or animating being or influence. I would like for you to consider it to be a supernatural being that inhabits a place, *your body*. It has the power to provide wisdom. The sooner you connect to this guidance, the quicker you will learn that all power does not rely with you. Develop your inner spirit through awareness and continuously seeking the presence that provides a level of knowledge beyond your capacity to understand.

There is also the creation of *team spirit* that gets everyone in-tune. Create a team spirit by relying on others to share their skills and knowledge to help the group. Inspiring others is a charismatic trait that is a part of a leader's style. Creating an atmosphere where everyone is free to share, grow and have fun, while helping with the most impossible mission. But, tapping into this stream of knowledge provides you assistance with the other two platforms, Mind and Body.

Mind

Let's start once again with you. Nourish your mind by gaining knowledge through education. Education should not be considered a choice, but **mandatory** for success. Completing the basic education, graduating from high school, is a must. The next level could vary by your career choice. Remember the importance of "feeding" your brain with new information. Consider your mind as the central processing unit of your body. You have to be careful what you put in it, how it is influenced, and how you train it. **Remember "GIGO", garbage in garbage out.**

A leader is not afraid to allow others to grow and know more than they do. It is not always the leader sharing the skills. There will be others who will know more than you do about getting a task accomplished. However, as a leader, you have to have the big picture or forward thinking as to what will come in the future or determine the trends. Stretch your mind and the minds of your people. **Status quo is a comfort zone.**

Body

The Spirit and the Mind help to guide the Body. If the first two are addressed properly, your body has a better chance of exhibiting the appearance you desire. Your appearance is important as a leader. From your clothes, to your smile, to your grooming, a leader should look the part. How well you treat yourself is always on display. Appropriate attire for the young man can be challenging. Trying to keep the balance with the latest trends may not display the image needed to be considered a leader. Select the garments and sizes appropriate for your body. Lastly, how you carry yourself should be polite, respectful, and with dignity. That transfers to the people you are leading, as well.

Just like the quarterback of a football team, you can work out, train and get your body in shape. However, if you do not study the play book, practice, and perform on game day, the probability of receiving the trophy is very slim. The team has to perform. Regardless of the type of team you have or the reason the group is needed, everyone has to do their part. Keep an eye out for when others are feeling tired, down, or losing stamina. Ensure there is a balance in work, rest, and play.

So far, we have discussed the foundational structure of leaders and how it transfers to the followers, but there are principles to be applied, as well. So, what else makes a good leader? There are principles that help to fine-tune your leading ability.

Principle 1: Know Who You Are.

You cannot expect to lead others until you know who you are and that you are capable of leading your life successfully. There is much focus on knowing your ancestor's history. But much of the research can begin with knowing the results of your SWOT. A leader knows who he is… the strengths, weaknesses, opportunities, and threats (SWOT). This can prepare you for life challenges. In the chart below, fill it in to determine the results of your SWOT.

Strengths	Weaknesses

Opportunities	**T**hreats

Conducting assessments will help acknowledge the many facets of you, such as your skills, personality type and values. There are some additional tools that will help you determine these vary things. The Keirsey Temperament Sorter is a tool used to determine your personality type. Go to www.keirsey.com and complete the free online version. This tool has been proven to be quite accurate. Knowing your personality type can prepare you to relate to others, and know what it takes for you to operate successfully.

An assessment is also available to determine your interest inventories. Do you have what it takes to do what you want to do? Just because you do not have it now does not mean you cannot get it. Having this inventory list will help determine what career areas are best suited for you. The resource to assist with this is a book by Richard Nelson entitled *What Color is Your Parachute?* Not only will you find out more about what you want to do, but how to accomplish these desires. Values are tied to your desires. You are communicating your values everyday. There is another assessment that takes inventory of what motivates you. Often, we think we know ourselves, but can't figure out how we find ourselves in certain situations. There is another resource that you can try for free. Complete the value questionnaire at: http://www.mrs.umn.edu/services/career/career_planning/valquestion. php. You will focus on what is important to you, and what you may want to consider changing.

What does the ultimate YOU look like? Describe who you want to become. The more detailed you are, the easier it will be to apply the principles. Let's have it! What does your future picture of success looks like?

The Future You

Career:_____

_____

Family:_____

_____

Financially: _____

_____

Lifestyle: _____

_____

Education: _____

_____

Emotionally/Spiritually:_____

_____

Health:_____

_____

Community: _____

_____

Now I am sure you are wondering how this all ties back to leading others. The very exercise you went through with this principle you can also do with your followers, to some degree. You need to get to know each one of them so you can assist them in any way possible.

> "I have heard it said that the first ingredient of success - the earliest spark in the dreaming youth - is this; dream a great dream."
> —John A. Appleman

Principle 2: Have a Vision and Personal Mission.

Leaders have vision. They do not follow all people. Having foresight of where you want to go helps you to follow those who have achieved this, or will put you on the right path. You have addressed the many aspects of your life in "The Future You" section. Now, think of one or two sentences that summarize the view of your future. Write it here.

_____

_____

What you have just created is a personal vision statement. This statement is now your guide for your life. Can you adjust it? Of course! It is meant to provide direction to guide your days, decisions you make, and choices you make about life. It is now your walking billboard. Every well-known product has a brand, and you know it when you see it! You are now building your personal brand. Let's go a step further into the vision.

Can we be real for a minute? I am sure you have heard that women mature more quickly than men. The verdict is still out on that, but from my personal opinion, there is some truth to that phrase. Let's take a little test to determine if there is some validity to the maturity level difference. Be honest. Don't ponder the answer; give your first gut-feeling answer.

Have you been spending more time playing your Playstation 3, Wii or electronic toy more than figuring out your strategy for life after your secondary education?	Y	N
The lyrics to the latest hits have been telling your life story and the videos have helped you determine your next move?	Y	N
Getting your buzz on and landing the attention of the hottest girl in school has become your mission.	Y	N

If the answer to any of these questions is yes, you may want to pay particular attention to this section of the chapter. Let's really focus now on your plan for your life. In this section, you will set goals and intermediate steps. In this chapter, you have created your vision statement. Are your actions supporting this vision? A leader ensures that all that they do helps to support the cause, the vision. How do you plan to get there? You need a plan. Let's focus on a plan for your life.

You need goals and intermediate steps. Again, your vision will not occur just because you wrote it. There has to be **action** behind it. Fill in the blanks below.

Long-Term Goals

Where do you see yourself in 10 years? Put an actual date here:

_____

Goal 1:_____

_____

_____

When? _____

What will I need? _____

Who do I need to help me? _____

What will it cost? _____

How will I do it? _____

_____

How will I celebrate? _____

Goal 2:_____

_____

_____

When? _____

What will I need? _____

Who do I need to help? _____

What will it cost? _____

How will I do it? _____

_____

How will I celebrate? _____

Short-Term Goals

Where do you see yourself in 5 years? Actual date in five years:

_____

Goal 1:_____

_____

_____

When? _____

What will I need? _____

Who do I need to help? _____

What will it cost? _____

How will I do it? _____

_____

How will I celebrate? _____

Goal 2:_____

_____

_____

When? _____

What will I need? _____

Who do I need to help? _____

What will it cost? _____

How will I do it? _____

_____

How will I celebrate? _____

Goal 3:_____

_____

_____

When? _____

What will I need? _____

Who do I need to help? _____

What will it cost? _____

How will I do it? _____

_____

How will I celebrate? _____

If you think just getting this far in the chapter was hard work, wait until you start putting this into action. The next principle focuses on building and honing some key skills.

"The man without a purpose is like a ship without a rudder – a waif, a nothing, a no man."—Thomas Carlyle

Principle 3: Equip Yourself and Others.

You have to get the influence before you get others to follow. There has to be something about you to make others want to join in on a mission. At the same time, there will be others that will want to challenge you. If you are not strong enough in knowing who you are, they can make you lose your confidence in your leadership position. The way to handle this is not guns, murder, fighting physically, drugs or suicide. It is fighting with skills that can be used as your weapons.

The equipment you will need is universal to any leader. Challenges will come, life will happen, and choices will be made both good and bad. You must have determination, self-discipline, and love yourself unconditionally. Let's take a look at each one.

Determination

There is a popular saying that, "Life is not easy." There are challenges in life and there are good times. In order to achieve and lead, you must be determined. Consider this: there is a level of difficulty that happens to everyone in life. Even men that come from a two parent household, limited financial challenges, and family history of highly educated men have had problems come their way. It is all in how you respond to them. You can't lose hope along your way. You have to keep your eye on the trophy and achieving your vision.

Deal with the issue by figuring out what may have caused the situation, and then what it will take to get back on track. This is the same thing you would do if an issue arrived in a group you were leading. The blame game just delays progress. Figure how you got there, develop a plan of action, and include a strategy to prevent the situation from reoccurring. Followers are looking to you to keep them focused and motivated. You lose sight and they will, too! The mission will be lost. Stay the course.

Self-Discipline

Don't let your power to influence and lead go to your head! One of the biggest challenges those in power face is not abusing their position. Controlling your desires and wants are very important. There are benefits and perks to a top position, but using them in the wrong way will hurt your credibility. Again, it comes back to you. Others will be watching what you do and say. Make sure you are disciplined in action and deed. You have the authority to make decisions and affect others. Remember, you do not have to make *all* the decisions.

You can empower your followers to make decisions. However, not before you have ensured that they are disciplined. Allowing them to make decisions or overseeing tasks means you are transferring some of your power to them. They are, in fact, representing you. Viewing their personal accountability to self-discipline will assist. The very thing you viewed within yourself can be applied to them. This leads to the final principle.

Principle 5: Hold Yourself and Others Accountable.

A part of being disciplined is being held accountable. Your parents are accountable to you. The teacher is accountable to the students, parents and school system. CEOs of companies are accountable to the board of directors and shareholders. Accountability is a part of the checks and balances of systems. However, accountability is not a bad thing! It ensures performance, goals, objectives, and that tasks are completed. As a leader, you are accountable for the well-being of your followers and those you report to. Here are some accountability rules for you and your followers:

- Value others.

- Keep your word to the best of your ability.

- Set high expectations for yourself and others.

- Give consistent, meaningful, and constructive feedback.

- Maintain rules, laws, and guidelines that have been established.

- Instead of giving excuses, make them lessons learned.

- Take action and execute.

- Know and accept the consequences for all your actions.

Leadership is not just a position, but it is also a journey. **Leadership is as leadership does.** John Quincy Adams has been quoted as saying, "*If your actions inspire others to dream more, learn more, do more and become more, you are a leader.*" You have been provided with much to do and maintain. Just remember, all that has been shared in this chapter is not all there is to learn about leadership. Continue to expand your mind and read constantly so that you are aware of your leadership potential, and chart a course to assure that you are a strong, accountable leader who will inspire many.

Reading Resources:

The Leadership Challenge by James Kouzes and Barry Posner

Seven Habits of Highly Successful People by Stephen Covey

ABOUT THE AUTHOR

AMICITIA MALOON-GIBSON

Amicitia Maloon-Gibson is the President and Founder of ATIC & MG Center For Excellence (MGC4E), Inc a non-profit community base global training and service institute. The focus is on Education, Empowerment, and Encouragement to Excel – E4 for human capital. Maloon-Gibson & Associates is the profit entity of the MGC4E. She has developed, implemented and delivered seminars and workshops in the United States and in International countries. Additionally, Cita brings 25 years of experience working with government and private organizations in the areas of leadership, training, motivation, team building, employee recruitment & succession planning, and organizational development. She has a Bachelor degree in Psychology and a Masters degree in Management and a Masters degree in Human Resources Development.

She is a member of the American Association of Christian Counselors (AACC), the Black African-American Christian Counselors (BAACC), the Marriage and Family Network (AACC) and she is a certified Mediator/Life Coach. She is a charter member of the Brevard County Business and Professional Women/USA/FL.; National Association of Female Executives, the Association for Conflict Resolution. She is a member of Women Speakers Bureau and a 29 years Veteran of the U.S. Armed Forces. She is a Board of Director member of Christian Services Charities for 2008-2009.

Cita Maloon-Gibson delivers exceptional seminars and keynotes, and is available for regional, national, and international travel engagements. Her international travels include the British Virgin Islands, US Virgin Islands, England, Germany, Prague, France, Belgium, Puerto Rico, Hawaii, Aruba and the Bahamas.

Contact:
Amicitia Maloon-Gibson
P.O. Box 411482
Melbourne, FL 32941
(321) 537-5002
Maloon57@aol.com
www.citagibson.com
www.mgc4e.org

TWENTY-ONE

RESOLVING CONFLICT

By Amicitia I. Maloon-Gibson

"The Lord is compassionate and gracious; slow to anger, abounding in love." (Psalms 103:8) KJV

I believe that the world is full of conflict. Conflict is manifested in many places, such as school, church, business, communities, and yes, in our home. In today's society, if you look at television you can see various forms of conflict or hear rumors of conflict. Most of the rumors of conflicts we see in foreign countries like Iraq and Afghanistan we call "war." Hollywood produces some products, such as movies, videos, games and DVD's, and distributes them in nice packages that depict and carry conflict into our homes – it is called entertainment in our society.

No, you cannot hide from conflict, for it will find you sooner or later. And if you say "I don't have conflict", I say keep living and be prepared to resolve it when its path finds you. What is your definition of conflict? Merriam Webster dictionary defines conflict as competitive or opposing action of incompatibles; antagonistic state or action; mental struggle resulting from incompatible or opposing needs, drives, wishes, or external or internal demands. Sounds like a recipe for a Jambalaya. It's a mixture of emotions, positive and negative, which can affect you externally or internally. Young men do have emotions, now given a popular title, by Bishop Theodore Dexter Jakes, as "HEmotions," which is also the title of one of his books. It is a choice or a decision you make to "act" on conflict in a positive or negative way.

I believe that the world is comprised of people who want to live a harmonious and peaceful life. We can agree to disagree; however, we must determine what the "root cause" of the disagreement is, and resolve them by considering all sides and to develop an acceptable solution. As you step out on center stage on the journey of becoming a successful young man, you will encounter conflict. A time will come when you reach a decisive moment, and it will be up to you to make a decision to act in a positive or negative way.

Let's look at the word "resolve". My definition, in simple terms, is to clear up or work it out successfully. Merriam Webster's definition that I chose to use is to reduce by analysis; deal with successfully; clear up or find an answer. What is your definition of resolve? In pursuit for success, your character, integrity, honor and values are a critical part of who you are and what you will become as a young man. Great leaders, pastors, politicians, generals, teachers, even your parents and myself, have experienced conflict. Conflict is inevitable, and it will come your way, good or bad. My question to you is, how will you resolve it? The choice or decision you make will determine the results you will get. I am here to suggest to you a few Self-Assessment Exercises that can help you identify the "root cause" of conflict, and present some strategies to resolve conflict and alleviate unnecessary stressors in your life. Resolving conflict can help you to have a healthy lifestyle and live a holistic and abundant life towards success.

"Keep thy heart with all diligence; for out of it are the issues of life."
(Proverbs 4:23) KJV.

Keep in mind that what you see, hear, and speak affects your emotions (attitudes and behaviors). This is what I call the SHS formula. As a young adult, I learned quickly that I had to change my environment that was creating conflict in my life. I had to guard my heart. So my SHS was selective. Friends that bullied me or called me names were no longer in my circle of influence. I used my strengths to counter the conflict. That is, I got good grades, new friends, and chose not to respond negatively to the name-calling.

It's not easy, but you can overcome conflict with love. Thanks to my loving Father for saying these powerful words of encouragement to me, "Love those that despitefully use you." He constantly reassured me that Daddy Loves you, and Love concurs all. He gave me a song to keep in my heart, and to guard it when conflict or challenges arise. As I reflect, I hear him: he speaks, I hear him and I see him. He was changing the way I think, and teaching me about life. Changing the way you think about conflict, or anything, will give you the results you need to be successful in today's society.

Before you can influence anyone to change the way they think, we must first "know thyself." Meaning, we must get a better understanding about ourselves and about our knowledge on the subject. Teachers and professors call this a pretest to assess how much you know or don't know about the subject. Psychologists and Counselors call the process an assessment tool. Regardless of what it is called, the purpose is to get a better understanding about "yourself" through fact-finding and soul searching. I would like you to complete the following three Self-Assessment Empowerment exercises, which will assist you in finding the "root-causes" of conflict in your life. Be honest with yourself and don't be afraid of the results, because you will have some strategies to assist you in resolving conflict in the early stages.

Self-Assessment Empowerment Exercise 1:

My definition of conflict is:

_____

_____

_____

_____

_____

My definition of resolve is:

_____

_____

_____

_____

_____

Self-Assessment Empowerment Exercise 2:

Reflect on past experiences and situations involving conflict and answer the following questions:

1. What are the causes of conflict in my life? (Be honest with yourself.)

_____

_____

_____

_____

_____

2. Who is causing conflict in my life (list friends, family, health, teachers, etc.)?

_____

_____

_____

_____

_____

3. Why is the conflict – conflict? (Identify the situations and what happened.)

_____

_____

_____

_____

_____

4. What was the behavior/emotion(s) that caused the conflict in my life? List at least five. (i.e. jealousy, lack of communication, sibling rivalry, missing parent, lack of resources, other imposed indicators)

_____

_____

_____

_____

_____

5. What action(s) did I take to resolve or not resolve the conflict?

_____

_____

_____

_____

_____

6. What are some skill sets, methods, and strengths you used to resolve conflict?

_____

_____

_____

_____

_____

7. List some skills that you have observed others using to resolve conflict that was effective.

_____

_____

_____

_____

_____

It is important in resolving conflict that you identify the "root cause" to be able to resolve the real indicator(s) of the conflict. Attempting successful conflict resolution requires actively "listening to" all parties involved and providing an opportunity for all parties to participate. As a Mediator, I have resolved and settled many disputes and employment complaint cases. It required me to listen for several hours to all parties. Mediation involves having a neutral third party resolve or settles your dispute. In some instances, it could be a teacher, parent, clergy member, or another neutral party. Professionals in Conflict Resolution seek to get win-win results for parties involved in the dispute, versus obtaining a win-lose situation.

Years ago, I enjoyed watching the Andy Griffin Show. Whenever conflict arose in the town of Mayberry, the deputy sheriff, Barney Fife's famous quote was, "Andy, we've got to nip it." That is the goal in resolving conflict to process the resolution in the early stage, "nip it". On your journey to success, you want to resolve the conflict and not dissolve the relationships. Building relationships and being a team player is another key leadership trait you can place in your toolkit for becoming a successful young man. Below is an exercise of Self-Assessment for journaling daily and documenting your conflict, the behavior, and the outcome of the conflict for seven days. What did you see? What did you hear? And what did you speak (SHS) in your life?

Self-Assessment Empowerment Exercise 3:

Journaling for seven days, how do I understand my behaviors and indicators of what causes my conflict (root causes)?

Reflection (What happened?)	Responding/Emotions (What Skills did you use?)	Results (What was the outcome?)
Day 1		
Day 2		
Day 3		
Day 4		
Day 5		
Day 6		
Day 7		

By now, you are probably wondering what all these Self-Assessment Empowerment exercises add up to? It's the summation of the people, things and behaviors that triggers emotions in you to cause conflict. Being able to defuse, resolve, or end a situation requires and understating of what the "it" is. When you can identify the "root cause", you can resolve the key conflicts in your life by changing your thinking and/or your behavior in a given situation, and by changing your environment.

Changing your environment could mean changing jobs, changing where you live, and sometimes may involve changing your "Circle of Influence." Remember what I said before, that you will have defining moments, and at these crossroads in your life you will have to make a choice, good or bad.

It is my hope that, with these assessment empowerment tools and exercises, you would avoid the latter. It is imperative that you understand who you are and what role you partake in a conflict situation. Why? So, that you will use an appropriate approach to resolve it quickly. Conflict is not all bad, and it can be used to stimulate new ideas, creativity, and affect change and more effective life strategies for your success as a young adult male. Briefly, for understanding - conflict may occur within the individual, between individuals, and between an individual and a group or groups. The types of conflict can be generalized into four key areas:

<u>Types of Conflict</u>

    1. Intra-personal

    2. Inter-personal

    3. Intra-Group

    4. Inter-Group

Intra-Personal Conflict

This is self-producing conflict that may lead to a diverse variation of complication. (Some examples: unnecessary worrying, anxiety, stress or illness.)

Inter-Personal Conflict

A situation that evolves conflict between parent and child, husband and wife, or relatives in general and friends. (Some examples: value differences, personality differences, or it could be a simple difference in communicating.)

Intra-Group Conflicts

Conflicts that occur between individual and a group. (Fraternity President and members of the fraternity, choir director and choir members.)

Inter-Group Conflict

Conflicts that occurs between two or more groups and the groups' members.

An Approach to Resolving Conflict

As a Parent of two teenagers, challenges and conflict occasionally occurs. What I know for sure is that with teenagers, you must "listen" actively to the messenger. Many parents and teenagers frequently find themselves in conflict with each other. From my experience in working with youth and family disputes, mediation is the chosen alternative that facilitates a healthy communication dialog for both parents and teenagers relevant to their issues. Mediation offers the family unit faced with conflict with an option to facilitate understanding in order to resolve the issues at hand.

I come from the generation of Baby Boomers (old-school). During my up-bringing, the mediator was the "Village", meaning everyone who told you to do something was right. You dared not contradict or discuss that the adult was wrong (unless you were in an unsafe environment). Mediation is most useful in situations when behaviors of youth or teenager exhibit indicators of escalated systemic issues within the confines of the family unit.

Conflict Resolving Styles

Maya Pilkington, author of *Test Your Business Skills*, describes the following styles that people adopt to resolve conflict:

The Brick Wall Approach: When a conflict looms, the brick wall type withdraws behind personal defenses, refusing to get involved.

The Ramrod Approach: The ramrod type builds up steam to force the issue. He fights and tries to dominate the situation because he will feel weak if he loses an argument.

The Feather-Bed Approach: The feather-bed type gets out the metaphorical oil to pour on the troubled waters. He hates to see anyone in conflict, and tries to smooth ruffled feathers and makes soothing noises.

The Compromise Approach: The compromiser hates extremes. He looks for the middle ground, and expects to give up something in order to gain something.

The Wise Old Bird Approach: The wise one spends time to resolve conflicts, confronting all the issues with courage and the clear intention of learning something in the process.

So, what can I do as a young man in the meantime, who is in the middle of a conflict? I am glad you asked. In simple terms, to encourage all parties in the conflict to stop doing everything else and shift their energies and focus to understanding three areas of their relationship by asking and answering these three critical questions:

1. What am I failing to learn from this conflict?

_____

_____

_____

2. What can I do to understand the others better?

_____

_____

_____

_____

3. What are the conditions that are creating the problem behavior we are all involved in?

_____

_____

_____

_____

Understanding the real problem apart from its symptoms is a tried and true problem-solving strategy. This is because understanding any problem is three-quarters of its solution. Fixing symptoms in conflict isn't the help that is needed, because that approach doesn't work. The only thing that does work is to take the time and make the commitment to truly understand the conflict and the people who are in it. That process always starts with understanding the difference between what you think you want to get out of the resolution, and what the conflict can teach you. The bottom-line to all this is - that understanding leads to acceptance, and acceptance opens the door to seeing a creative win-win compromise to end the deadlock.

At times, we make the simple things in life too complicated. The book of work may be easier to read than we want to imagine; but maybe that is because we don't want to know the ending too soon, for fear of not having enough to do.

Self-Assessment Empowerment Exercise 4:

Taking Ownership of Your Conflict

Were you the "root cause" in some of your relationships that involved conflict?

Relationship	Root Cause Person

Now, take the posttest. Go back to the pretest and see if you would answer each Empowerment Self-Assessment Exercise differently. Now that you can identify "the root causes" of conflict(s) in your life, what are you going to do?

Write it here, as you journey on your path to becoming successful:

_____

_____

_____

_____

ABOUT THE AUTHOR

SHANNON JONES, RN, BSN, MAOM

Ms. Shannon Jones is the President and Chief Executive Officer of CNS Services, Inc. She has served in the healthcare industry for over 20 years has been in leadership positions for 14 years including Chief Operations Officer and Director of Patient Care Services at Healthcare Organizations in diverse geographic areas within Los Angeles and Riverside County. She earned a Masters degree in Administration and Organization Management (MAOM). Ms. Jones' primary motivation for forming her consulting company was to provide a range of educational and training programs which would allow organizations and individuals, achievement of goals and personal excellence.

Shannon Jones offers professional and personal development training programs to a variety of businesses, healthcare organizations, individual coaching, and education for youth. With her passion and commitment to improving team work, self esteem and communication, Ms. Jones continues to inspire and train hundreds of individuals from multicultural backgrounds to embrace new opportunities for leadership, personal and professional development.

She makes available educational material and practical methods to implement effective changes and encourages positive decision skills that lead to greater work performance and self confidence.

Ms. Jones continues to be an active professional leader and lecturer. Some of her honors include:

Keynote speaker for Compton Adult School graduation, Keynote speaker for Harriet Tubman Teen Mother School graduation, andKeynote speaker for the Sweet Hour of Prayer Faith Christian Center "Women Conference".

Shannon Jones' experience and wisdom provides evidence that challenges are opportunities for success. She is a Certified Coach, motivational instructor and a dynamic speaker. Her managerial experience and love of people allows her to "connect" with her audience. Put this all together and you have an excellent formula for success.

Contact:
CNS Services, Inc.
PO Box 90218
Los Angeles, CA. 90009
(310) 639-5461

TWENTY-TWO

LEARNING TO FORGIVE

By Shannon Jones

Forgiveness Relating to Health

Perhaps one of the most vital lessons in life to be learned is one that can never be taught, but attained through the personal and emotional choice of forgiveness. Forgiveness is defined as the act of pardoning somebody for a mistake or wrongdoing (Encarta Dictionary), but it entails so much more than just its definition. Forgiveness is, in fact, an exercise of the mind's right to allow the spiritual, emotional, and physical states of the body to be at harmony and on one accord. Thus meaning that when a person chooses to clutch on to unforgiveness, he is allowing himself not to be healthy, as total health is defined and broken up into three components: mental/emotional, physical, and social. In order to be deemed a healthy person, the three components of health must at hand. When an individual chooses not to forgive, it affects the emotional factor of health, usually causing stress and anguish. This can lead to an disruption of the physical element of health, often causing the body to go in a state of dire health as a result of high blood pressure, or other health problems related to stress. In fact, forgiveness has been found to be a coping strategy minimizing rage and hostility (Al-Mabuk, R.H., R.D., & Cardis, P.A., 1995 *Journal of Moral Education*). Unforgiveness can be as addicting as drugs, alcohol or overeating. It acts as a silent killer, desecrating the mind, and generating a void in the human soul. Unforgiveness has often been the root of conflict, causing broken relationships, human spirits, physical illness, and broken hearts. Therefore, it is important to exercise a forgiving persona in order to be in complete health.

Identifying the Root and Learning to Forgive.

Forgiveness is in the "Control" of the individual. It is a choice, one that cannot be forced or coerced, but given freely, both internally and externally. Nevertheless, before the decision is made either to pardon or to hold a grudge (a feeling of resentment or ill will, especially one lasting for a long time, *Encarta Dictionary*), one must first discover and examine the root of the situation that seeks forgiveness. In doing so, this will allow the person to call to mind the situation and its effect, and explore what could have been done differently, thus using problem solving techniques to come to a verdict.

The power to forgive lies within each of us, and when it is in demonstration, you create a powerful force to be reckoned with. Abraham Lincoln once stated, *"Am I not destroying my enemies when I make friends of them?"* Forgiveness brings freedom; it is the act of releasing yourself from past unpleasant experiences, thus reestablishing control over your life. Henceforth, one of the first steps that you will need to take in order to promote healthy living is to learn how to forgive. When you learn to forgive, you begin to heal and reconnect with a healthier outlook on life, and liberate yourself from self-destruction.

Learning Self-Forgiveness

So, now you understand why forgiveness is important, as it relates to emotional and health reasons. Now, the next step is for you to deal with the pain. In other words, you have to be true to yourself, and acknowledge your true emotions surrounding the event and or person that created the painful experience. Do not try to minimize your pain because it is very real to you. If you do not go through this process, you will undermine your goal of truly releasing this negative energy, thus defeating your purpose of being healed. Emotional pain can show up in a variety of areas in your life, such as your health, weight loss and or gain, excessive drinking, and drugs, just to name a few. Once you have acknowledged your feeling and release the pain, forgive yourself. Yes, forgive yourself. A large reason for us to hold on to forgiveness is that it allows us not to take responsibility for our own actions and emotions. So, go ahead and forgive yourself, and began to take comfort in the fact that you did your best with the knowledge you had at that time. Therefore, free yourself from self-hatred, anger and pain.

Exercise:

What have you done that created a reason to learn to forgive yourself?

_____

_____

_____

Forgiving Those Who Do Us Harm

One of the most difficult decisions for us to make is the choice to forgive those that have harmed us, whether the effect be physical, psychological, emotional, or social, when we have experienced harm at cause of another individual, particularly those in close relations. It is tougher for us to understand their reasoning for hurting us, and usually more difficult to forgive that person. As victims of the hurtful dealings of others, several of us struggle with crippling feelings and aftereffects of the tactless actions of others. However, it is of great importance that we choose to pardon those that do us harm. Booker T. Washington said, "*I shall allow no man to belittle my soul by making me hate him.*" By not forgiving others who have wronged us, we ultimately hurt ourselves by harboring negative thoughts evoking negative energy leading to possibly an increase in the stress levels in the human body. Lewis B. Smedes stated, "*Forgiveness is the key that can unshackle us from a past that will not rest in the grave of things over and done with. As long as our minds are captive to the memory of having been wronged, they are not free to wish for reconciliation with the one who wronged us.*"

We must learn to forgive and release the resentment in order to progress internally and externally. Harboring unforgiveness blocks that growth and development we need to succeed in life and learning to cope with the pains we experience is apart of developing. Dr. Joan Borysenko (*Fire of Soul*) stated, "*Forgiveness is not the misguided act of condoning irresponsible, hurtful behavior. Nor is it a superficial turning of the other cheek that leaves us feeling victimized and martyred. Rather, it is the finishing of old business that allows us to experience the present, free of contamination from the past.*"

Who must you forgive who has harmed you?

_____

_____

_____

The Burial

The next step to take is to allow yourself time to grieve, and have your burial service, because sometimes pain comes in a form of rejection, lost, and betrayal. These feeling can create such a strong feeling of depression and sadness that it will consume your life. If we will be honest with ourselves, most of us attempt to suppress our negative feelings in regard to others because we are taught it is wrong to let people see you in pain, because it is perceived as weakness. The damage physically, emotionally and mentally is great when we deny ourselves the opportunity to grieve over a loss. You become stoic, and declining to express your feelings will not release you from your emotional pain; it only causes you to delay your healing process. Therefore, acknowledge your pain, forgive yourself, and have your burial.

Exercise:

How have you been hurt? What happened?

_____

_____

_____

How will you conduct your "burial" for this pain?

_____

_____

_____

Here are some things to think about when you have hurt someone else and have not forgiven yourself (buried your pain):

Remorse vs. Spite:

1. Did you hurt someone purposely or accidentally?

2. Accept responsibility.

3. Reach out to the other person with an apology.

4. If they accept it, feel the peace.

5. If they do not accept your apology, do not become spiteful. Express your apology and feel the peace.

6. Forgive yourself for hurting the other person. Be certain that you have learned from this, and choose not to repeat the behavior.

7. If someone has hurt you and chooses not to apologize, forgive them anyway. Feel the peace. Rather than becoming spiteful, consider whether they hurt your purposely or accidentally. Also consider if they hurt you repeatedly. If so, forgive them, but distance yourself from them. Do not allow someone else to control your emotions. Release yourself from the shackles of being emotionally bound to this person. Let go of the pain and wishing for "payback". Move on with your life.

Understanding Your Own Beliefs and Value System

Forgiveness and moving on in life is complicated for everyone. However, the spiritual and psychological reason must be recognized as well, because these painful experiences threaten our relationship to life itself. Dr. Caroline Myss, (in her book *Anatomy of the Spirit*) stated, "*When we harbor negative emotions toward others or toward ourselves, or when we intentionally create pain for others, we poison our own physical and spiritual systems. By far, the strongest poison to the human spirit is the inability to forgive oneself or another person. It disables a person's emotional resources. The challenge is to refine our capacity to love others as well as ourselves, and to develop the power of forgiveness."*

To release and move forward is the act of accepting what is considered injustice, according to human thinking. Forgiving and moving forward is the act of accepting that a Divine reason exists within the unreasonable, and even within the most horrific experience, along with the reality that we will never know that reason. Yet, the truth is that, regardless of what happens to each of us, the choices we have are to hold on to the pain and remain empty, or let go.

Forgiveness is the act of retrieving your spirit from your history with the intention of opening to grace and direction for the future. No answer will ever satisfy that quest. Using such a direct and powerful imagery as confronting the memory directly in front of you is a way of breathing your spirit back into your body, drawing your energy out of the trauma (not your memory, but your energy), and consciously committing your spirit to reshape your present moment. Doing this exercise is a measuring device that allows you to assess how much of your energy still lives in the past. Each time you tackle the images, breathe your spirit back to present time, adding the prayer that grace reshapes your present moment and fills it with tranquility, acceptance and endurance.

When you find your mind slipping into the sadness created by the weight of personal tragedy, immediately focus your attention on your breathing, repeating to yourself, "I am remaining in present time and I am invoking the grace to prevent me from sinking into the weight of yesterday." A constant desire to remain in present time rebuilds your spiritual reserves, slowly and continually. Eventually, there will come the moment when the energy in that reserve tips in your favor. Then, when your soul feels its' strength returning, then call the image forward one more time with the intention of retrieving the remaining fragments of your spirit.

Many times you might feel that when you forgive the person, you now have to continue the relationship. You do not have to. It is your choice. Forgiveness does not necessarily mean the relationship must be completely restored. However, you will have to examine yourself and how much you value the relationship in order to determine whether it can be completely restored.

On a personal note, I strongly believe that there are certain relationships that cannot only be fully restored, but become even stronger and more loving than before the painful experience took place. In order for this to happen, it takes unconditional love and true commitment from both parties. In the words of Dr. Martin Luther King Jr., *"Forgiveness is not an occasional act; it is a permanent attitude."*

Notes:

_____

_____

_____

_____

_____

_____

_____

_____

_____

_____

_____

_____

_____

_____

_____

_____

_____

_____

_____

_____

_____

_____

ABOUT THE AUTHOR

MICHELLE BRYANT

Michelle Bryant, President and CEO of M. Bryant & Associates, has developed seminars to bring awareness to the lifestyles for the times in which we live. With issues as diversity, racism, and aging revolving around us daily, there is a need for understanding. Ms. Bryant has developed life skills through her experience in diverse working and living situations, and imparts her wisdom to others on focusing on our positive traits. Her life experiences, co-existing in different regions, and witnessing certain behavioral rituals have given her seminars a sense of reality and humor. As we all know, laughter cures the soul. Bryant brings real life experiences to her seminars with seminar topics including: eliminating poisonous relationships, diversity, branding and image. She is a certified Diversity Trainer as well as Professional Life Coach; however, Ms. Bryant prefers the term "Life Stylist"

Ms. Bryant has studied under Linda Ellis Eastman, Founder and President of PWN, and is co-author of Self-Esteem and Empowerment for Women. She has completed training in Image Consulting in New York City, and is certified in make-up artistry. Ms Bryant has had the pleasure to be a guest on The Magnolia Show, the first radio show to be dedicated to women's market in the state of Florida, and hosted by co-author Nyda Bittmann-Neville.

Contact:
M. Bryant & Associates
7212 Reading Road, Suite#1
Cincinnati, Ohio 45237
513.252.1969
Lifestylist101@aol.com

TWENTY-THREE

AVOIDING POISONOUS RELATIONSHIPS

By Michelle Bryant

Avoiding poisonous relationships is not an overnight assignment; it is a job. People can push your emotional buttons, but your knowledge of handling these Poisonous Relationships ("PR" as we will refer to in this chapter) and recognizing the signs of unhealthy behavior, will assist you in reacting in a healthy way. The word Poison is defined as "something destructive or harmful." If this word describe a relationship you are involved in with a family member, significant other, friends, or business co-worker, beware that "PR" can stir up unhealthy behavior. Keep your focus on your success.

When you think of people with whom you share a "PR", who comes to mind? List their names, and their relationship to you.

1. _____

2. _____

3. _____

4. _____

5. _____

You had no control over your life as a child, and may have participated in, and witnessed, dysfunctional "PR". List the person and event:

1. Physical abuse: _____

2. Sexual abuse: _____

3. Emotional abuse: _____

4. Rage: _____

5. Beating: _____

6. Humiliation: _____

7. Sarcasm: _____

8. Envy/jealousy: _____

9. Silent treatments: _____

10. Neglect: _____

11. Possessiveness: _____

12. Absolute control: _____

13. Disrespect: _____

14. Manipulation: _____

15. Sabotage: _____

Perhaps one of the most profound products of witnessing "PR" as a child is carrying this behavior into your adult life. This may occur because of:

- Your witnessing of your parents unhealthy marriage

- Your witnessing of parents in relationships with no stability

- Lack of a positive male figure or role model in the home

- Lack of your basic needs being met (food / shelter)

- Not let alone

When you become used to unhealthy behavior, it is easy to enter into a "PR". You may have poisonous ways of communicating with others. Be aware that you may execute some of the same unhealthy behaviors that you witnessed in childhood, as we know children imitate or mimic what they witness in their environment. When you become involved in personal relationships, you may be over-possessive, manipulative, jealous; you basically become the abuser in the relationship, if you have witnessed that behavior at home. But, you have the power to re-design your relationships!

Here are some of the thoughts and feelings of unhealthy behaviors that may have followed you into adulthood:

- Fear

- Abandonment

- Anger

- Lack of trust

- Guilt

- Paranoia

- A need for control

Exercise:
Ask yourself these questions:

Why are you friends with people that have unhealthy behaviors?

_____

What emotions do you feel when you interact with these people?

_____

Are these emotions you feel positive or negative?

_____

Do these emotions interfere with your ability to be a better you?

_____

The word " trait" is defined as "a distinguishing quality (as of personal character)." Here are some traits of unhealthy behaviors:

1. No compassion, lack of respect of family, authority figures, etc.

2. Violence-driven decision making

3. Don't value life as much as they should

4. Bad reputation, known as a trouble maker, drug user, criminal

Associating with these unhealthy behaviors will never inspire you or motivate you to become the powerful and magnificent man you can be. Well, it's not too late for you to Re-Design your Style! The definition of Re-Design is, "to revise in appearance, function, or content." Execute your plan to change your life! Talk with a mentor, pastor, or someone that you RESPECT for advice on habits you may need to change.

You must have a map, some sort of directions, to get to a destination. The same is true in real life. Where is your map? Have you designed your chart of destiny? When you get side tracked or run into situations that seem difficult, handle them, move on, handle the next task, stay focused on your positive energy. You are responsible for designing the map of your life.

Start with these steps of Re-Designing your relationship with yourself:

• Talk to yourself with positive words, hype yourself up, amp your energy. (Tell yourself to GO FOR IT!)

• Treat yourself and others with respect (girls/women/elders).

• Eliminate as much negative energy as possible.

• Don't let negativity make your decisions.

• Bring positive energy into your life and thinking.

• Find your passion.

- Read the Bible. It is full of the histories of surviving against all odds.

- Pray, meditate.

- Laugh/smile (Looking angry does not show confidence.)

Top professional men, such as sport figures, entertainers, writers, authors, CEOs, are men who have learned to deal with "PR"; they have focused on their mission to succeed, eliminating "PR". These men show confidence by smiling and being positive. So, start smiling, because it could be your secret weapon!

The best way to eliminate "PR" is to begin with yourself. Start having a healthy relationship with yourself and others. Appreciate the people who appreciate you. Eliminate those who bring you down or poison your world and dreams. Create a life for yourself where you can reach your destiny with the help of positive, supportive people who are emotionally healthy.

Notes:

_____

_____

_____

_____

_____

_____

_____

_____

_____

_____

_____

_____

_____

_____

_____

_____

_____

_____

_____

_____

_____

ABOUT THE AUTHOR

Dr Teresa Kasey-McClendon

Teresa Kasey- McClendon, Ph.D., is a respected educator in both the Christian community and the public educational system; she is a motivational leader, as well as mentor to women and youth. She is the Founder & Co-Pastor of The Way Life Message Center & Training Institute, Inc & Co-Founder of The Way of Life Family Worship Center International Ministries located in Boynton Beach, Florida and is a native of Roanoke Virginia.

She is a former Licensed Missionary in the Church of God in Christ, and has held such positions as the District Elect lady of the Evangelist Department in the Greater Western District. Dr. Kasey- McClendon was also chosen to host Southwestern Virginia's First NAACP Awards Affair.

Dr. McClendon is involved in the development and training of outstanding leaders. She works cooperatively and collaboratively with organizations, groups, and individuals to increase knowledge and skills in a manner that allows participants to blend them effectively to the richness of diversity, while using her resources to help all to achieve sustainable growth, effectiveness, and competitiveness.

Dr. McClendon is currently a member of The Professional Woman Network National Speakers Bureau and has recently founded"The Message Center & Training Institute for Women". Dr McClendon's love for youth led her to start an outreach ministry entitled Champion Builder's Youth Mentoring Program which is in partnership with The National Mentoring Association, and the Inspiration for You Women's Outreach Fellowship, located in South Florida. She is married to Pastor Michael J. McClendon and the mother of (2) daughters Tierra and Kimberly. A Wife, A Mother, A Pastor, A Mentor, and a Friend.

Her academic credentials include a Ph.D. in Christian Education and an Ordained Pastor & Evangelist. She holds certifications in such fields as Evangelistic Training Association Instructor, Effective Black Parenting, and Women's Issues. She is a Certified Professional and Personal Development Educator and Trainer, a Certified Diversity Educator, and Certified Youth Relations Trainer.

Contact:
The Way Life Message & Training Center
Email: liv2livagin@aol.com

TWENTY-FOUR

THE MISSING INGREDIENT: A MOTHER'S TOUCH

By Dr. Teresa McClendon

Society today, and in the past, has stated that we are a product of our environment. This message is what is driven into the minds of humanity, especially into the minds of our young men of today. As we look around, resentment to this statement is very evident; however, when we really take the time to analyze this synopsis, it is unbearably true. Men as well as women are products from whence they came, and it does not take a rocket scientist to discover such a reality. On the other hand, our male species must learn young that, even though their environment has labeled them, the power to change is still available. He must realize that where one starts is not where he will necessarily finish. If you do nothing to change your course in life, then you will remain the same, and your environment will speak for you. Once the male reaches the age of adulthood and in his mind begins to establish in his own heart who or what he desires to become, he will then begin to strive diligently to obtain the path to a life of success.

In order to be successful in life, one must possess insight to many principles and have access to wisdom keys. Nurturing with wisdom is a preservative that, when applied to a productive male life, brings forth balance and a strong and stable foundation. This wisdom and insight must be available at all times, starting from infancy (a state of helplessness) to adulthood (a place of mature decision-making). We want to make sure that our young men are clear about the "Stages of Enlightenment for a Successful Life." Many fail to realize that their geographical location or level of income does not determine who they are or what they will become. It is the desire to obtain wisdom, along with the ability to pursue knowledge and understanding for the necessities of life. Therefore, once the male begins his journey to gain wisdom and insight, he must not over look the nurturing component. He will conclude that it resides in the Mother's Touch, filled with lots of love and compassion.

The wisdom that the Mother's touch possesses is the ingredient that gives flavor and consistency to a well-rounded life.

I would love to say that it is the father's visit to the baseball games, or him buying the shiny red wagon, the summer evenings fishing on the riverbanks, or even hiking the highest mountains together that brought about life-changing insight. Nevertheless, I would be amiss if I did not bring your focus back to the importance of the words of wisdom and empowerment that are embedded in the depths of the **wise mother**.

Some can remember when their baseball team lost the game and they wanted to quit, and how Mom made you feel like you were still the winner. Perhaps you wrecked your bicycle and you did not want to show the fear that accompanied the fall, but mom convinced you that it was healthy to express those feelings, and taught you how to conquer them. What she taught you gave you the strength to try again. Some could even attest to the times when they admitted that they didn't particularly like the feeling of worms, and would rather not indulge in the sport of fishing at all. They would rather stay home and wait for the hot cookies from the oven and that cold glass of milk as they had long talks with Mom as she baked. Choosing to watch cartoons, rather than being made to feel bad about not having the desire to take that long tedious hike up a steep and dangerous mountain. Speaking of which, you never really understood why people took the time to climb, anyway.

The decision not to partake of the things you had no interest in was accepted by Mom. Wisdom explained what was best to choose for your interest. This insight, along with so much more, can be located in the ingredients of the wise mother; these mothers were designed to encourage and give wisdom to all who listened. This wisdom flows out of her compassion and desire for the success of a child. What I love about it is that it does not just have to be her child, but any child. With every wise mother, there are set principles and goals to live by. The mother laborers to build character, striving to make a boy into a dependable man, and a prince into a reigning King, while at the same time teaching him how to rejoice and live life to its fullest.

One can easily identify an individual with these traits of success. Their life will exemplify the very essence of one who has encountered the ingredients of a wise mother, and reveals that they have embraced her principles without hesitation. These signs, just to name a few, are visible due to their overwhelming rewards in life. At one time or another, each has been the tool used by the wise mother to train her children into vibrant citizens in today's society. We must all agree that the major necessities of life consist of:

1. Food

2. Clothing

3. Shelter

4. Education

5. Financial Resources

6. Love

7. Transportation

8. Communication

We all then must agree that education is essential to life, and may be retrieved from many resources. A mother's wisdom is a resource, tailor-made to the characteristics of a particular individual that is to be enlightened. To refuse to take advantage of the opportunity to learn from the teaching of a mother, or to refuse to seek out your source for wisdom, is to accept failure.

Many may reply that their mother was not in their life to impart wisdom, for one reason or another. Whatever may be the case, there is still hope.

*"Excuses are merely the nails that build the house of failure,
a place we should never live."*—Author unknown

I want to refresh your memory as to how I purposely stated earlier that a mother's wisdom is not only for her own child, but also for children in general. So, I admonish you not to allow this to be an excuse not to seek out a mature woman to mentor you. Someone, another other than your biological mother, can and will freely impart the wisdom, love, and compassion you need to become a mature young man.

A part of the wise mother's very nature is to educate, build and strengthen for the generations to come. Below are a few brief statements to assist in identifying a few principles of a mother's wisdom (the missing ingredient).

A Few Principles of a Mother's Wisdom.

- Always seek to complete what you start.

- Always walk upright in integrity.

- Work hard for what you desire, and never look for handouts.

- Always save for a rainy day.

- Think of the consequences before accepting the quickest way out.

- When you do not know what to do, do not do anything until you are sure of the right thing.

King Solomon is one whom the Bible considers the most wise man in the world. He is known for writing the book of Proverbs. One of the proverbs reads as follow:

"My son, observe the commandment of your father and do not forsake the teaching of your mother." —Proverbs 6:20

Many fail to realize that to be able to teach your children wisdom is an immeasurably significant privilege. This privilege builds a successful and prosperous Stage for Life. King Lemuel wrote the last chapter of Proverbs, but he credits his mother with the wisdom contained in his words. Whereas most of Proverbs deals with a father speaking, chapter 31 contains a mother's wisdom and her characteristics. Her words to her son deal mostly with the contrary things that life offers that will take a young man far off the path of success. King Lemuel advises his son to listen continually to what he is commanding him, and to what his mother is instructing or teaching him, and never depart from her words.

Take some time and list situations you have already encountered that will keep you from a Successful Stage in Life. Write down how you plan to fix each situation:

1. _____

   _____

2. _____

   _____

3. _____

_____

4. _____

_____

5. _____

_____

Examples of situations young men encounter in life that keep them from experiencing the successful stages in life are:

- Continually surrounding oneself with people who have no desire to possess a successful future.

- Allowing your environment to change you, opposed to changing your environment.

- Fear to pursue your dreams of success.

- Settling for opportunities that generate quick revenue, in which the ending result brings life altering consequences, i.e., theft, selling of narcotics, or gambling, etc.

- Establishing a stable foundation for life, before pursuing self-fulfillment.

Where there is a strong and plentiful resource for life's necessities, the opportunity for success is phenomenal. It is when the resources have ceased, or cannot be located, that the onset of real dilemmas occur. This reading is important because many young men feel that their chance for mentoring through a wise mother has passed them by. However, the moment you decide to reach out for impartation, you will receive exactly what you need.

There is some woman waiting on her 'son' to find her so that she will be able to pour into him the years of experience and insight she has gained just for him. She desires to share with him all that she has learned, and to encourage him that, even though there is a big world before him with lots of choices, it also presents many opportunities. With the right guidance and support, nothing is impossible, and anything he applies his heart, mind and ability to, he can achieve. From infancy to adulthood, the wisdom of a mother is such a great and needed ingredient. We must come to the place of enlightenment and knowledge that, without the wisdom of a mother, presidents could never rule nations, judges would never judge fairly, and doctors could never heal their sick with compassion.

Remember the love of a mother and the wisdom that accompanies her is yours for the asking. It is very important that you seek out your mentor while planning your path to success. Let's look at some traits of an excellent female mentor.

Traits of an Excellent Female Mentor:

• Someone that is loving and not judgmental.

• A nurturer

• Someone with a positive outlook on life.

• Someone who walks in integrity.

- Someone with insight to everyday living.

- Someone independent; and yet knows how to use life's resources.

- Someone who's willing to give of herself, without looking to receive in return.

- Someone who is God-Fearing and knows the principles of Godly living.

Some fail to ask questions or to be direct when inquiring about their mentor. So that you can appreciate the value of a female mentor, several questions need to be answered within your own mind. Take some time and answer these questions listed below, and if you feel the need for assistance, seek out a successful male who has a positive female role model in his life.

What exactly do you need from a female mentor?

_____

Who are some of the positive female mentors recognized in the 21st century?

_____

What qualities do you need to enhance in your life, and how can a female help you?

_____

Do you need a hands-on mentor, or would you rather select one from a distance?

_____

What are your views on women leading or educating men?

_____

Refuse to sway towards negative insight or persuasion. When it comes to women mentoring young men, remember that women are nurturers who are able to assist you in becoming successful in life. Whether it is your mother, sister, aunt, or even a complete stranger of the female gender who is willing to educate and assist with reaching your full potential in life from the perspective of a woman, she should be classified as a valuable commodity and be treasured for life.

Notes:

_____

_____

_____

_____

_____

_____

_____

_____

_____

_____

_____

_____

_____

_____

_____

_____

_____

_____

_____

_____

_____

_____

ABOUT THE AUTHOR

TRACEY MORRIS

For the past ten years, Tracey has been training business leaders and organizations to tap into the instinctive talents of their employees, develop high-performance teams, improve productivity, and facilitate better communication and improved relations at all levels of the organization. Tracey conducts leadership and management training workshops, develops training and performance development programs, and provides personal coaching for business managers. Her expertise lies in identifying communication breakdowns in organizational structures; then develops programs and practices to improve effectiveness.

Tracey is the Development Services Manager for Samtec, Inc. a global manufacturer of P.C. Board level interconnects with over 2,200 associates worldwide. In this capacity, Tracey spends most of her time working one on one with managers and associates to achieve personal and professional growth through self-awareness and behavioral change. Her true passion is helping people get what they want. She contributes to Samtec's organizational development initiatives and is the architect of Samtec's training approach.

Tracey is a certified consultant for Kolbe Corp, Inc., Phoenix and has specialized training in NLP and mediation techniques. She holds a B.A. degree in Organizational Management from Midway College and is a member of Professional Women's Network. She is a native Kentuckian and lives in Louisville.

This chapter is dedicated to her son, Peter Ballman.

Contact:
Tracey Morris
Tracey.Morris@insightbb.com
(502) 896-2806
(502) 338-6280

TWENTY-FIVE

WHAT IS A MAN?

By Tracey Morris

There are millions of men of all ages living on our planet. They live their lives daily according to their own culture, traditions, religions, values and beliefs. They live their lives as men based upon how they were raised by their parents (or parent) and the influences they received from families, community, schools and churches. All can significantly influence a young boy's attitude about adulthood.

Ideas about what a man should be, or could be, flow from society through media, arts and technology. Regardless of where a young man lives in the world, these influences are within reach and make a powerful impact.

Also, each person is born with abilities and attributes unique to them. These are the things about us we can't really explain other than to say: "It's just who I am."

When you, as a young man, identify a role model from personal encounters through the outside world or within yourself, the image can have both positive and negative qualities. Both men and women influence you. Because there are so many influences and options for a young boy, finding a correct answer to the question 'What is a man?' is a challenging exercise. The answer is both *individual* and *universal.*

This chapter is a two-part exercise.

Part one is the *individual* piece of "Who do I want to be as a man?" You will explore personal experiences with other family members, community, school or church, and also ideas from society at large. You will form an image of a man based on, 1) what you have learned from personal relationships with men and women in your life up to this point, 2) the characteristics you think a man should possess and not possess based on society, and, 3) an exploration of the unique abilities and attributes you were born with and want to develop further.

Part two is the *universal* piece of 'What do I want as a man?'. This is actually a theory open for discussion: regardless of where a man lives in the world, he wants to achieve three things: independence, financial freedom, and satisfying relationships. There are three activities related to achieving these: setting goals, generating options, and having a vision (dreaming). The relative importance of part two will vary based on your own culture, tradition, religion, values and beliefs, but it is an exercise worth doing to decide how it fits into your own answer to the question: "What is a Man?"

PART ONE – Individual Role Models

1. Personal Relationships and Role Models

Regardless of age or country, boys learn from families and friends what they want and don't want to be as they evolve into manhood. In the English language, titles are used to describe men and women who are family members or friends. (Insert your own language for similar titles). For men, some titles are Dad, Father, Poppa, Granddad, Brother, Cousin or Uncle. For women, some titles are Mother, Mom, Grandma, Sister, Cousin or Aunt. Outside of family, some titles used are coach, teacher, or friend. These titles generate memories of people who have made a positive or negative impact to your world.

As a *positive* role model, he or she may have taught you a new skill or helped you learn how to handle a difficult situation. Maybe he or she treated you with respect and love. Perhaps he or she made you laugh. Whatever the reason, these people did something extraordinary to make you say, "I want to be like him", or "I want to be like her."

Based on titles and names, who are the people who have influenced you in a *positive* way, and how do you want to be like them?

Who has given me positive memories?	How do I want to be like this person?
1.	
2.	
3.	

Just as people can be positive role models, there are some we remember because they had a *negative* impact on our world. Never underestimate the power of a negative influence. They serve as a cautionary example of mistakes we don't want to make. Maybe it was someone too tough or too aggressive or too arrogant. Perhaps they criticized or embarrassed you. They may have been untruthful or reckless. Whatever the reason, they did something to make you say, "I don't want to be like them."

Based on titles and names, who are the people who have influenced you in a *negative* way, and how do you *not* want to be like them?

Who has given me negative memories?	How do I *not* want to be like this person?
1.	
2.	
3.	

2. Characteristics From Society (Media, Arts, Technology)

Men have many qualities and do many things. Men are often described as decisive, analytical, athletic, and strong. In the modern media (TV, radio, movies, internet, books, magazines, etc.), we place value on males (and females) who win, take risks, are physically fit, adventurous and brave. We encourage males to compete, excel and win. We discourage them to cry, get hurt or make mistakes. Yet, males are human beings who feel all emotions. Sometimes a man wins; sometimes a man loses. To live a successful, happy, productive life, and deal with the victories and failures everyone experiences, there are many characteristics a man can possess. Just as you learn from family and community (Exercise 1), you also get ideas from media and society about what a man should be. These role models can be both *positive* and *negative*, too.

Based on people you watch or read about in the media (TV, radio, movies, internet, books, magazines, etc.), who do you think is a positive role model, and how do you want to be like them?

Who do I think is a positive role model?	How do I want to be like this person?
1.	
2.	
3.	

Based on people you watch or read about in the media (TV, radio, movies, internet, books, magazines, etc.), who do you think is a negative role model, and how do you *not* want to be like them?

Who do I think is a negative role model?	How do I *not* want to be like this person?
1.	
2.	
3.	

If there are other *positive* characteristics you think are important for a man to possess, add them now: _____

_____

If there are other *negative* characteristics you think are important for a man <u>not</u> to possess, add them now: _____

_____

3. Unique Abilities and Attributes

Each human being is born with unique abilities and attributes. These abilities and attributes are like no one else. Even though you may look like, and sometimes act like, other family members, you are uniquely *you*. Think about easy and fun activities. You may have a unique ability to read music, pitch a baseball or make art. You may have a unique ability to remember numbers, do math in your head or learn languages. If it is easy and comfortable for you to tell jokes or make friends easily, it is probably because you are a happy person, have confidence in yourself, or like to say nice things to others. Unique abilities and attributes sometimes get lost in our thinking because we focus too much on things we *aren't* good at in life. To keep a healthy balance, it is important to give more time and energy thinking about, and working on, the things we *are* good at in life. When you think about your good points, you become a more positive person. Positive people create opportunities and possibilities for their lives because they believe in themselves, others and the world. Think about your unique abilities and attributes and write them down.

What are my unique abilities and attributes I want to develop more as I become a man?	
Abilities	Attributes

Now, you have completed Part One – the individual piece. Look at everything you have written about your personal relationships and role models, the role models from society, and your own unique abilities and attributes. Can you begin to see your own picture of what you could be, and should not be, as you grow into manhood?

Pull all of your ideas together from the three exercises in Part One and create your answer to the question: "What is a Man?"

The man I want to be will:	The man I want to be won't:

Today, this is your picture of the man you want to be. Your picture may change over time as people come and go in your life and leave an imprint on you. You will also change as you learn more about yourself through experiences and relationships.

PART TWO – Universal Achievements

Regardless of where a man lives in the world, he wants to achieve three things: independence, financial freedom and satisfying relationships. Even if it sounds unrealistic right now to think of yourself as independent and financially free, what you do and think about today helps you build a foundation to achieve both. Even though we make our own choices throughout life, we depend on others for support, guidance and friendship. So, developing and maintaining satisfying relationships with a variety of people will enrich you. Enjoying independence, financial freedom, and satisfying relationships are all within reach. To get there, you need to a) set goals, b) generate options and c) have a vision. Let's briefly discuss these three activities.

People who *set goals* and write them down (this is important) almost always get what they want. When you set a goal and write it down, you are making a commitment to yourself and have some confidence in your ability to achieve the goal. Goals require thought and consideration. Before a goal becomes clear in your mind, you usually think about options.

Generating options is all about ideas. It starts by asking yourself, 'What if...?' You will need a flexible mind to get better at generating options. A flexible mind thinks in terms of possibilities instead of thinking about what cannot happen. At the same time, options must be realistic. For example, you can't drive your car to school if you are only fourteen years old! When you generate options, you are optimistically thinking about all the ways you might achieve your vision for the future.

To have a *'vision for the future'* is an adult way to describe 'dreaming'. Too much daydreaming leads to inaction, but active dreaming about the future is required before you can generate options and set goals. When you dream, you ask yourself, "What do I want to have happen?"

Let's look at the three universal achievements and see where you are today. Then you can fast-forward to the future for each one, generate options and set short-term goals as you build your own foundation to achieve independence, financial freedom and satisfying relationships. Once you do this process, you can repeat it again for long-term goals or short-term goals as many times and as often as you want.

1. Independence

Being independent means doing things on your own and in the way you want to do them. It involves making decisions about your life with what you do, what you believe, and what you think. Independence is a big responsibility. It means you have to 'own' yourself by taking responsibility for your actions and thoughts. Sometimes, it's when we are alone and on our own we learn the most about ourselves.

Right now, you are probably more independent than you think. Even if you live at home, there are ways you are independent. You may walk to school or take care of your brothers or sisters. You may fix your lunch or cook meals. Certainly you make decisions with your friends. If you decide to go with them to a movie, or if you decide not to go, you are expressing independence. If a friend or acquaintance laughs at someone else's misfortune, and you don't think it's funny, you are expressing your independence.

Today, how am I independent?	

When we think about the future, we usually consider 'short-term' and 'long-term' possibilities. Think about the next year (short-term). How would you like to take more responsibility for yourself and express more independence?

In the next year, how would I like to become more independent?
1.
2.
3.

For each item listed above, think about options and ideas to help you achieve your vision for more independence.

What options do I have to become more independent?
1.
2.
3.

Now that you have thought about what you want and generated options for getting what you want, clarify your thoughts by writing down your specific goals to become more independent in the next year.

In the next year, these are my goals for demonstrating more independence.
1.
2.
3.

2. Financial Freedom

Financial freedom means paying your own way. Total financial freedom means to have no debt. If you want to go to college, purchase a home, or buy a car, it is difficult to think it is achievable in most economies without borrowing money from a bank. In some cultures, going to college, purchasing a home, or buying a car isn't important or even possible due to government or economic realities. Whatever the situation exists for you due to culture or beliefs, financial freedom means you are no longer reliant on anyone else to pay for basic needs: food, shelter and transportation. It means you have the money to take care of your own needs and those of your family, if you decide to have one. When a man enjoys financial freedom, it opens up a larger world of possibilities in which to enjoy life and living. Financial freedom doesn't mean a person is a millionaire. It means a man spends less than he makes and has the financial resources to generate more options in his life.

Right now, you may bring financial resources to your life. You may get paid for doing chores or babysitting. You may receive a weekly allowance from your parents or have a part time job. One way or another you have money in your pocket from time to time. Sometimes money is given to you for birthdays, special occasions, or just because someone wants to give it to you. But, when you receive money on a regular basis without earning it, there is a potential danger of becoming dependent or coming to expect it. If you receive money without earning it, make sure you express gratitude to the person giving it and recognize it as a temporary situation. Financial freedom is realized by your own hard work, receiving an income, spending wisely, and saving for the future. It is your responsibility to pay your own way.

Today, how do I bring financial resources to my life?	
1.	
2.	
3.	

When we think about the future, we usually consider 'short-term' and 'long-term' possibilities. Think about the next year (short-term). How would you like to take more responsibility for your finances?

In the next year, how would I like to become more financially stable?
1.
2.
3.

For each item listed above, think about options and ideas to help you achieve your vision for more financial freedom.

What options do I have to bring financial resources to my life?
1.
2.
3.

Now that you have thought about what you want and generated options for getting what you want, clarify your thoughts by writing down your specific goals to bring financial resources to your life in the next year.

In the next year, these are my goals for bringing financial resources to my life.
1.
2.
3.

3. Satisfying Relationships

A satisfying relationship means having someone you can count on. It's the person you care about who cares about you. Let's face it, no one can live entirely on their own without building a relationship with someone. You build relationships by treating others like you want to be treated, by doing what you say you are going to do, and generally being honest, trustworthy, and expressing gratitude to those who help you. Not everyone you meet will become your close friend, but certainly everyone you meet has something to teach you. Relationships, whether close or distant, will impact and influence every aspect of your life: physical, spiritual, mental, financial, social, family.

Today, what relationships are important to me?	

When we think about the future, we usually consider 'short-term' and 'long-term' possibilities. Think about the next year (short-term). How would you like to develop or improve your relationships and with whom?

In the next year, what relationships would I like to develop or improve?
1.
2.
3.

For each item listed above, think about options and ideas to help you achieve your vision for developing and improving your relationships.

What options do I have to develop better relationships in my life?
1.
2.
3.

Now that you have thought about what you want and generated options for getting what you want, clarify your thoughts by writing down your specific goals to develop and improve relationships in your life in the next year.

In the next year, these are my goals for developing relationships in my life.
1.
2.
3.

You have completed both parts of this chapter. Congratulations!

Now, you can see the pattern of how you are evolving into a man, your own man. You are a composite of your role models, personal influences and society. You have your own unique abilities and attributes with your own dreams and goals for achieving independence, financial freedom, and satisfying relationships. This may be the beginning of your search to answer the question 'what is a man?', but you now have a process you can use throughout your life to identify and evaluate what you are learning from each person who influences you. Evolving as a human being is a lifelong experience. So will your evolution into becoming a man. What kind of man do you want to be?

ABOUT THE AUTHOR

DANETTE WOODS MORRISON

Danette Woods Morrison has been an educator for over 15 years both in Louisiana and Texas. She is certified to teach 4th through 8th grade Social Studies and is a certified Parent and Youth Trainer. Ms. Morrison is a graduate of Louisiana State University where she received her B.A. in History with a minor in Broadcast Journalism. LSU was also the place where she met her college sweetheart Derrick, now her husband. They have been married for 15 years and have three beautiful princesses Jovanté, Derrianna, and Derriane.

Danette believes that education begins at home and teaches each of her students as if he or she is her own. She is a member of the National Council of Social Studies and constantly looks for innovative ways to teach her students so they may experience success in their lives.

Due to Hurricane Katrina, Danette and her family were forced to leave their hometown of New Orleans and place their residence in Houston, Texas. She states "As a hurricane survivor, I am not a victim and I refuse to allow my circumstances to dictate my future." Danette firmly believes and stands on "with God ALL things are possible." She thanks God for her family who instilled in her hard work ethics and a "don't give up attitude."

She is currently working on starting her own consulting practice, becoming a motivational speaker and writing children's books full-time. At present, she's the co-author of "Louise's Hairy Adventure".

Contact:
Danette Woods Morrison
14515 Briar Forest Dr.
Houston, TX 77077
(281)759-5564
(504)301-6661
urtyme2travel@sbcglobal.net

HANDLE YOUR ANGER OR IT WILL HANDLE YOU

By Danette Woods Morrison

"In your anger do not sin. Do no let the sun go down while you are still angry, and do not give the devil a foothold."—Ephesians 4:26-27, NIV

If you have found yourself saying, "I've gone too far. I wish I would have listened. If only I had walked away before things had gotten out of hand. Why can't I control my anger?" Truly, you have experienced anger. This emotion is a part of your daily life, but how you handle it will determine the outcome of the goals you are trying to achieve.

There are two common types of anger: visible and invisible.

Visible anger is that aggressive behavior where you see a person acting out in a way that normally causes harm to themselves, others, pets, and/or property.

Example 1:

Jeff's parents will not allow him to use the car to go to the basketball game. He goes to his room, slams the door, and kicks the cat. While he's in his room, Jeff throws things around and shouts how much he hates his mom and dad. Then his dad steps into his room and informs him that not only is he not allowed to use the car for the night, but for the next month. Jeff is also not allowed to go anywhere and he has to do extra chores around the house.

Identify Jeff's goal.

_____

_____

Did Jeff achieve his goal?

_____

_____

Invisible anger is the type of anger that normally catches everyone off-guard. This is the anger where a person suppresses that anger and is likened to a time bomb. This type of anger has built up over a period of time and is waiting to explode at any moment.

For three months, Marvin decided he wanted to make better grades and not get into any trouble, but some students had been making fun of Marvin. One day when Marvin walked in class, Antoine put his foot out and tripped him. Marvin stood up, fixed his clothes and sat down in his seat. Some of the students laughed. On another day, Marvin did not feel well, so he placed his head on the desk and went to sleep. Joseph, Antoine's best friend, decided to sneak up behind Marvin and hit him on the back of his head. Marvin jumped up immediately, but he only told Joseph to leave him alone. Some of the boys thought this was funny and called Marvin "weak", "soft", or even a "punk". On the day of standardized testing, the teacher noticed Marvin was acting really strange. She said Marvin seemed really agitated; he kept putting his hands on his head looking at the other students with disgust. At one point, the teacher said he wanted to walk around the class. In between testing, Alan made a comment about the test aloud, but not to anyone in particular. Marvin told him to shut up or he was going to beat him. Alan told Marvin to make him shut up. Before anything could be done or said, Marvin leaped from his seat and began hitting Alan repeatedly. It took three teachers and a police officer to break up that fight. Upon Marvin's return from his suspension, he told his teacher that he was disappointed with himself that he allowed the boys to get to him, and that he was trying to handle his anger by ignoring his classmates.

Invisible anger is just as dangerous as a loud outburst or display of out-of-control emotions. Because Marvin allowed his anger to build up, it came out at Alan, but he was really upset with Antoine and Joseph.

There are many reasons why you experience anger; whether it's self-inflicted, or against parents/siblings, friends, teachers or strangers.

Example 2:

When Jimmy was eleven, his dad used to abuse his mom. Jimmy was angry with himself because he didn't help her. At one point, he wanted his dad to leave, and he wanted his mom to stop doing whatever it was she did to make his dad beat her. He felt torn because he loved both parents, but did not know how to help either one of them. Jimmy then would come to school, disrupt class, make bad grades, and bully his friends. Ten years later, Jimmy was arrested for murder.

"Do no let the sun go down while you are still angry, and do not give the devil a foothold."

Was Jimmy responsible for his parents' actions? No. But, he internalized their problems and made them his own. This unresolved anger with himself and with his parents caused him to have failing grades in school, poor relationship with his peers, and behavioral problems, which led him to committing a crime that resulted in Jimmy spending the rest of his life in prison, or facing the death penalty. The case is still pending. Jimmy was not a bad person, he just needed someone to talk to and assist him in dealing with his situation.

Complete the assessment below. Circle the response that describes your actions when you are angry.

Have you ever punched the wall?				
Never	Rarely	Sometimes	Most of the time	Always
Have you used profanity when someone cut in front of you in line or while driving?				
Never	Rarely	Sometimes	Most of the time	Always
Have you ever thrown an object when your parents or guardian wouldn't allow you to have your way?				
Never	Rarely	Sometimes	Most of the time	Always
Have you cried when you failed a test or didn't get a promotion?				
Never	Rarely	Sometimes	Most of the time	Always
Have you kicked someone or something when your girlfriend broke up with you?				
Never	Rarely	Sometimes	Most of the time	Always

Have you ever raised your voice trying to get your point across to your friend?				
Never	Rarely	Sometimes	Most of the time	Always

Have you used obscene language when your boss/teacher accused you of something you didn't do?				
Never	Rarely	Sometimes	Most of the time	Always

Have you ever thrown your books when you failed a test?				
Never	Rarely	Sometimes	Most of the time	Always

Have you ever walked away from a fight or an argument?				
Never	Rarely	Sometimes	Most of the time	Always

Have you ever thrown your Gameboy or ball away when you lost a game?				
Never	Rarely	Sometimes	Most of the time	Always

If you have answered sometimes, most of the time, or always to any of these questions, there are some tools I'm going to give you to use, and show you how to enhance three important characteristics you may already possess. Trust me, you have the potential to achieve greatness; it just needs to be brought out of you.

How Do You Handle Anger?

I know it's a testosterone thing that guys have about expressing certain emotions. I've seen it because I've taught 6th through 8th grade boys, and the level of manly hormones were extremely high. On a daily basis, I explained to them that there are specifics that God intended to do to make them a male child. There was not/is not a need to constantly prove that you are a man with actions that result in bad consequences. When you find yourself in certain situations, there are critical steps that need to be taken before you get to a place of no return, and allow yourself to get side tracked by the foolishness. In addition to the other characteristics that make you who you are, you have to be a **self-managed, respectful gentleman.**

What is Self-Managed?

When you look at the word "self", it refers to you. It means that only you can control or direct you. Your ultimate goal for you is to always be in control of self. Notice, I did not say in control of the situation. Trying to control every situation will keep you frustrated. It is an impossible task to achieve; therefore do not waste your time.

Example 3:

A few years ago, my house was one of the many that were damaged by Hurricane Katrina. There wasn't anything I could do to prevent this disaster from taking place. My house flooded, and I had never experienced anything like that in my entire life. I could have allowed this whole ordeal control me, but one thing I knew without a doubt was that God is ALWAYS in control. Did I cry? Yes, I was angry. Did I cry a lot? Yes, I was frustrated, but I had to focus all of my energy on helping myself, as well as my family, get through this. We had to move to a new state, a new job, and my children were in a new school. We had to encounter people calling us names and telling us they didn't want us in their city. I could not go around beating up people who made me angry. This type of behavior would have been counter productive to what really needed to get done. I only answer to myself, and

I was none of those things they were saying. I couldn't allow myself to be a victim. I had to trust God and continue to pray. I thank God daily, because I know I survived for a reason. I couldn't possible walk around angry at the world all the time. What lesson would I be teaching my children?

If you are not self-managed, someone, or the situation, will manage you. Now, I'm not saying you shouldn't get angry; it is okay to get angry. Just don't go to bed angry or allow your anger to take you out of yourself. On the other hand, neither should you walk around as if you never get angry; that's an unrealistic way of life, and very unhealthy.

You can become self-managed when you are able to identify those things that set you off. We call those triggers. There are several things that may tick you off. So, here are a few for you to rank from 1 to 10, with 10 being the most:

__ Losing a game.

__ Someone accidentally bumps into you in the club.

__ Smashing your finger in a door.

__ Failing a test.

__ Unable to attend a friend's party.

__ Being stopped by the police without just cause.

__ Not getting the job.

__ A girl just told she does not want to go out with you.

Other triggers that are easily recognized are the abuse of alcohol, tobacco and drugs. Surely these negative actions result in negative consequences. Once you have identified your triggers, here are some tools you can use to become self-managed.

1. **Pray**. Praying ALWAYS works. "Lead you not in to temptation, and deliver you from evil." God gives you a way out of the trouble you are heading toward, or even when you're in it. You have to choose to accept your help.

2. **Self-Analysis or Self-Talk**. It **IS** okay to talk to yourself, especially if it's going to allow you to achieve your goals without any negative consequences, or does not cause any harm to anyone else. Examples of what you can say to yourself:

   a. "I am self-managed."

   b. "I am confident."

   c. State your goals. "My goals are…" Keep your eyes on your prize.

   d. "I can handle this. I am confident and calm in this situation."

3. **Pause and Take a Deep Breath**. Count to 10 or 20 before reacting. If you have to count to 100, by all means please do so.

4. **Make a Good Decision**. You need to make the right choice that will lead to good consequences.

5. **Talk to Someone Who's Not Involved in the Situation**. Here's another opportunity to pray and ask God to show you the right person to talk to. A person who is going to be honest with you, allow you to express yourself, and suggests some positive options.

6. **Avoidance or Retreat**. Walking away from a potential problem or backing down from one is being a self-managed gentleman whose goals are bigger than the situation at hand.

7. **Journal**. Write it down. Sometimes it helps to express yourself on paper rather than saying it aloud. This also allows you to take a second, third or fourth opportunity to rethink the situation, and maybe you can come up with a workable solution.

8. **Remain Calm**. Throughout the entire situation, remain calm. Once you have paused and taken a deep breath, say:

   a. "I am angry because....."

   b. "When you did or said...., I got upset because..." The most important point of this is to stay calm and watch your body language. Your body language can escalate or de-escalate the situation. If you normally express yourself with your hands, it may send the message that you may become violent. Look the person in the eye and speak as calmly as possible. **<u>DO NOT STARE</u>**! You know staring at someone indicates your "mean-mugging" them, and that's a sure way to get off track and away from your plans.

9. **Do Nothing**. Maybe some people are angry because of something in their own lives, and yet, their own anger was directed toward you.

Use this as a guide in becoming self-managed. BE HONEST!

I follow the rules at home and at school.		
Almost	Always	Work On It
I use my good listening skills.		
Almost	Always	Work On It

I do my assignments in a timely fashion.		
Almost	Always	Work On It
I work to the best of my ability. I ask for help when I need it. I do not copy anybody else's work.		
Almost	Always	Work On It
I work well with others.		
Almost	Always	Work On It
I can work alone without getting distracted.		
Almost	Always	Work On It
I behave myself even when no one is around me.		
Almost	Always	Work On It
I am self-managed and I use good manners.		
Almost	Always	Work On It
I respect my own property and the property of others.		
Almost	Always	Work On It
I don't hurt myself or others. I help others.		
Almost	Always	Work On It

What Does It Mean To Be Respectful?

As a self-managed gentleman, you have to be respectful, because being a gentleman means you possess that quality of being worthy of admiration. But, to add another quality to this also means you must be responsible. You have to take responsibility for your own actions. You cannot walk around blaming everyone else for what goes wrong in your life. When you admit you are wrong in spite of the consequences, you are well on your way to becoming a self-managed, respectful gentleman.

Example 4:

A 17-year-old young man met a girl online. They chatted for a couple of days and exchanged numbers.

Greg: Hello sir, may I speak to Sandy?

Dad: Excuse me? You want to speak to Sandy? Son, who are you and how old are you?

Greg: Yes sir. My name is Greg and I'm 17.

Dad: Where did you meet my daughter?

Greg: I met Sandy online and she gave me her number. We've been talking for about two weeks.

Dad: Do you know how old my daughter is?

Greg: Yes, sir. She told me she was 16 years old.

Dad: Greg, my daughter is 12 years old.

Greg: I apologize, sir. I didn't know and I won't be calling again.

What Does It Mean To Be A Gentleman?

The word "gentle" brings to mind "to handle with care." No, it **DOES NOT** indicate weakness in any form or fashion. What it does mean is that God has special plans for your life, plans to prosper you, and give you hope for your future. It is because of these plans that you cannot allow ANY ONE to bring out the worst out of you. As a gentleman, you must also possess the qualities of being honest, kind, and having integrity. You have to have strength, but not in an arrogant way. You do not have to walk around trying to prove how strong you are, but how caring and considerate you are. You must seek peace at all times. These are some of the qualities that make you a gentleman for yourself, and not just for the sake of a relationship.

Example 5:

The students were rushing into the building. Mrs. Lars was entering the building as well. She is not a favorite among the students, but Sam stopped, held the door open to allow her to go before him.

Handling Your Anger

Begin journaling those times when you were angry.

1.   What were you doing before you got angry?

2.   What was the problem?

3.   What caused the problem?

4.   What were your actions immediately after?

5.   What could have been done to avoid the problem?

6.   What physical changes took place before you reacted? (Facial changes, eye twitch, etc.)

7.   Identify the consequences of your actions before reacting. (Proactive, instead of reactive)

8.   What plan will you use to solve the problem?

Anger Outlets:

- Organized sports

- Weight lifting

- Golf

- Listening to music

- Taking time for yourself; relaxing

Once you have enhanced those characteristics of being a self-managed respectful gentleman, you should be able to recognize what triggers another person's anger, and you will avoid pushing their buttons. A self-managed, respectful gentleman takes responsibility for his own actions, and control of his own destiny. Go out and be the young man God intended you to be by making a positive difference in your own life and the lives of others.

Recommended Reading:

The 7 Habits of Highly Effective Teens by Sean Covey

104 Activities That Build Self Esteem, Teamwork, Communication, Anger Management, Self–Discovery and Coping Skills by Alanna Jones

THE PROFESSIONAL WOMAN NETWORK
Training and Certification on Women's Issues

Linda Ellis Eastman, President & CEO of The Professional Woman Network, has trained and certified over two thousand individuals to start their own consulting/seminar business. Women from such countries as Brazil, Argentina, the Bahamas, Costa Rica, Bermuda, Nigeria, South Africa, Malaysia, and Mexico have attended trainings.

Topics for certification include:
• Diversity & Multiculturalism
• Women's Issues
• Women: A Journey to Wellness
• Save Our Youth
• Teen Image & Social Etiquette
• Leadership & Empowerment Skills for Youth
• Customer Service & Professionalism
• Marketing a Consulting Practice
• Professional Coaching
• Professional Presentation Skills

If you are interested in learning more about becoming certified or about starting your own consulting/seminar business contact:

The Professional Woman Network
P.O. Box 333
Prospect, KY 40059
(502) 566-9900
lindaeastman@prodigy.net
www.prowoman.net

The Professional Woman Network
Book Series

Becoming the Professional Woman
Customer Service & Professionalism for Women
Self-Esteem & Empowerment for Women
The Young Woman's Guide for Personal Success
The Christian Woman's Guide for Personal Success
Survival Skills for the African-American Woman
Overcoming the SuperWoman Syndrome
You're on Stage! Image, Etiquette, Branding & Style
Women's Journey to Wellness: Mind, Body & Spirit
A Woman's Survival Guide for Obstacles, Transition & Change
Women as Leaders: Strategies for Empowerment & Communication
Beyond the Body! Developing Inner Beauty
The Young Man's Guide for Personal Success

Forthcoming Books:
Emotional Wellness for Women Volume I
Emotional Wellness for Women Volume II
Emotional Wellness for Women Volume III
The Baby Boomer's Handbook for Women

These books will be available from the individual contributors, the publisher (www.pwnbooks.com), Amazon.com, and your local bookstore.